总主编 文 旭

NEW WORLD
INTERACTIVE ENGLISH

新世界

交互英语
读写译 2 学生用书

主　　编：姜毓锋
副 主 编：彭兵转　李　雪
编　　者：（按姓氏笔画顺序）
马　亮　王泳钦　史　磊
孙　菲　陈福明　戚德山

原版作者：Milada Broukal

清華大学出版社
北　京

Copyright © 2017 by National Geographic Learning, a Cengage company.
Original edition published by Cengage Learning. All Rights reserved.
本书原版由圣智学习出版公司出版。版权所有，盗印必究。

Tsinghua University Press is authorized by Cengage Learning to publish and distribute exclusively this adaptation edition. This edition is authorized for sale in the People's Republic of China only (excluding Hong Kong SAR, Macao SAR and Taiwan). Unauthorized export of this edition is a violation of the Copyright Act. No part of this publication may be reproduced or distributed by any means, or stored in a database or retrieval system, without the prior written permission of the publisher.
本改编版由圣智学习出版公司授权清华大学出版社独家出版发行。此版本仅限在中华人民共和国境内（不包括中国香港、澳门特别行政区及中国台湾）销售。未经授权的本书出口将被视为违反版权法的行为。未经出版者预先书面许可，不得以任何方式复制或发行本书的任何部分。

"National Geographic", "National Geographic Society" and the Yellow Border Design are registered trademarks of the National Geographic Society® Marcas Registradas.

Cengage Learning Asia Pte. Ltd.
151 Lorong Chuan, #02-08 New Tech Park, Singapore 556741
本书封面贴有 Cengage Learning 防伪标签，无标签者不得销售。

北京市版权局著作权合同登记号　图字：01-2016-8559

版权所有，侵权必究。举报：010-62782989，**beiqinquan@tup.tsinghua.edu.cn**。

图书在版编目（CIP）数据

新世界交互英语. 读写译学生用书. 2 / 文旭总主编；姜毓锋主编. —北京：清华大学出版社，2017.3（2022.7 重印）
ISBN 978-7-302-46287-3

Ⅰ.①新…　Ⅱ.①文…　②姜…　Ⅲ.①英语—阅读教学—高等学校—教材　②英语—写作—高等学校—教材　③英语—翻译—高等学校—教材　Ⅳ.①H319.39

中国版本图书馆 CIP 数据核字（2017）第 020995 号

责任编辑：刘细珍
封面设计：子　一
责任校对：王凤芝
责任印制：丛怀宇

出版发行：清华大学出版社
　　网　　址：http://www.tup.com.cn, http://www.wqbook.com
　　地　　址：北京清华大学学研大厦 A 座　　邮　编：100084
　　社 总 机：010-83470000　　邮　购：010-62786544
　　投稿与读者服务：010-62776969, c-service@tup.tsinghua.edu.cn
　　质 量 反 馈：010-62772015, zhiliang@tup.tsinghua.edu.cn
印 装 者：山东临沂新华印刷物流集团有限责任公司
经　　销：全国新华书店
开　　本：210mm×285mm　　印　张：12.25　　字　数：345 千字
版　　次：2017 年 3 月第 1 版　　印　次：2022 年 7 月第 9 次印刷
定　　价：54.00 元

产品编号：071656-02

PREFACE

《国家中长期教育改革和发展规划纲要（2010—2020年）》明确指出，要"适应国家经济社会对外开放的要求，培养大批具有国际视野、通晓国际规则、能够参与国际事务和国际竞争的国际化人才"。《大学英语教学指南》提出，"大学英语课程应根据本科专业类教学质量国家标准，参照本指南进行合理定位，服务于学校的办学目标、院系人才培养的目标和学生个性化发展的需求"。

《新世界交互英语》是清华大学出版社站在国家外语教育与人才培养的战略高度，从美国圣智学习出版公司引进优质原版素材、精心打造出版的一套通用大学英语教材。为满足国内大学英语教学的实际需要，出版社邀请国内多所大学，在《大学英语教学指南》的指导下，对原版教材进行了改编。本套教材汇集全球顶尖品牌教学资源，贯彻启发性教学理念，以课堂教学为纽带，将全球化视野与学生真实生活联系起来，注重学生个性化发展需求，力求培养具有较高英语应用能力和跨文化交际能力的国际化人才。

一、教材特色

本套教材主要有以下特色：

❶ 素材来源：汇集全球顶尖品牌教学资源

本套教材的素材源自全球两大顶尖品牌教学资源：美国国家地理（National Geographic Learning）和TED演讲（TED Talks），为学生提供了大量原汁原味的视频、音频和图片，将世界各地的自然风光、风土人情、文化习俗带进课堂，以拓展学生的思维，并拓宽他们的国际化视野，从而达到提高学生语言应用能力和跨文化交际能力之目的。

❷ 编写理念：倡导启发性教学

本套教材将全球真实事件和精彩观点引入教学，结合中国传统文化和国情，注重思维训练，启发思考，以帮助学生理解中西文化差异，在培养学生听说读写译等英语应用能力的同时，着力培养其国际视野和创新精神，实现学生的全面发展。

❸ 核心目标：用课堂连接世界与学生生活

本套教材以课堂教学为纽带，将多姿多彩的世界万象与触手可及的学生生活连接起来，让学生具有全球化视野的同时，关注自身生活，思考中国问题，并学会用英语去表达自己的思想，从而成长为兼具扎实英语基本功和敏锐批判性思维的国际化人才。

二、改编思路

中方编写团队在对原版教材进行本土化改编过程中，做了适当的增补、替换和删减等工作。主要改编思路如下：

❶ 增补中国文化和中国国情内容

本教材注重培养学生对中国传统文化的认同，着力培养学生使用英语介绍中国文化的能力。在问题设计、练习改编方面重视本土问题，以帮助学生理解中西文化差异；在翻译、写作、口语活动中融入文化对比的元素，启迪学生对本土文化进行思考，培养其国际视野和中国情怀。

❷ 设计实用型和兴趣型练习

在设计练习时，适当参考了雅思、托福、大学英语四六级考试的题型，补充了更多的听力、翻译等练习，增强了教材的实用性；同时，结合时代发展，我们在"读写译"系列中加入扫描二维码以获取更多主题阅读材料的新元素，以充分调动学生的学习兴趣和求知欲望，使他们在主动学习的过程中提高英语水平和综合素养。

❸ 引入批判性思维训练和创新写作题型

本教材注重引导学生正确区分人物与观点、事实与解释、审美与判断、语言与现实、字面义与隐含义等，对问题进行批判性评价。"读写译"系列教材每个单元专门设计了一项针对批判性思维训练的练习，根据阅读模块内容启迪学生深度思考，进而提出独到见解；在写作能力培养上，设计了环环相扣、逻辑紧密的练习，体裁题材多样，积极鼓励创新写作，实现批判思维与创新写作的结合。

三、教材结构

本套教材分为"视听说"和"读写译"两个独立系列，每个系列包含学生用书和教师用书各四个级别。每个级别包含八个单元，每个单元可供四课时使用。

其中，"视听说"每个单元包含两大部分。第一部分主要围绕音频素材展开，包含A、B、C、D四个板块，分别对应四个教学目标（Goals）。第二部分的E、F两个板块主要包括视频素材和拓展练习，每个单元均包含美国国家地理录像视频Video Journal和拓展练习Further Practice，每两个单元之后含一个TED Talks视频。

"读写译"每个单元包含Reading、Writing和Translation三个部分。Reading部分包含两篇课文；Writing部分介绍若干个Writing Skills；Translation部分包含汉译英和英译汉两个篇章翻译练习。每个单元最后都设计了Weaving It Together综合和拓展板块，用以培养学生课下自学能力。

四、适用对象

本套教材适用于我国高校各层次公共英语和英语专业基础技能课程教学，同时也适用于成人自学。

五、编写团队

本套教材的总主编为西南大学文旭教授。"视听说"1-4册主编分别为莫启扬、孙阳、李成坚、段满福；"读写译"1-4册主编分别为崔校平、姜毓锋、刘瑾、马刚。来自全国近十所高校的几十名专家和骨干教师参与了本套教材的设计和编写，美国圣智学习出版公司的英语教育专家和教材编写专家对全书进行了审定。

在改编之前，我们广泛咨询了国内外英语教育领域的资深专家学者，开展了充分的调研和分析，确定了本套教材的改编理念和方案，最终使本套教材得以与广大师生见面。教材的改编凝聚了诸多专家学者的经验和智慧。在此，对为本套教材的改编和出版付出辛勤劳动的所有老师以及出版社的各位同仁表示衷心的感谢。由于水平有限，不足之处在所难免。我们真诚地希望大家提出宝贵意见，并在未来的修订中使之更趋完善。

文旭

2017年2月

UNIT WALK-THROUGH

Stunning **National Geographic images** introduce the unit theme and readings.

Theme-based units combine reading and writing through a balanced and engaging process designed to integrate the two effectively.

Pre-Reading activities prepare students by introducing key concepts and vocabulary from the readings.

Engaging readings motivate students to become better readers.

Post-Reading vocabulary activities recycle target vocabulary, building students' word knowledge.

Students look for the reading's main ideas and details to develop **key reading skills**.

Critical Thinking section challenges students to analyze, synthesize, and critically evaluate ideas and information in each reading.

Unit Walk-Through   v

UNIT WALK-THROUGH

Writing Skills provide students with essential tools for composition.

Writing Practice section activates the writing skills taught and guides students through the writing process.

Translation section provides two C-E and E-C passages related to Chinese culture, helping students develop their translation skills and intercultural competence.

Weaving It Together section includes Unit Project and Internet research activities, as well as extra theme-related readings, expanding students' knowledge of the unit theme and further developing their reading, writing, and research skills.

Unit Walk-Through   vii

CONTENTS

UNIT 1 Symbols
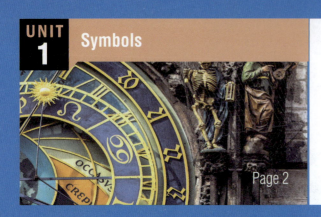
Page 2

- **Reading 1** Color Me Pink
- **Reading 2** And the Lucky Number Is...
- **Writing** Paragraph Structure | The Parts of an Essay | The Thesis Statement
- **Translation**
- **Weaving It Together**

UNIT 2 Customs

Page 24

- **Reading 1** Thanksgiving—Hawaiian Style
- **Reading 2** Hop to It!
- **Writing** The Introduction | The Conclusion
- **Translation**
- **Weaving It Together**

UNIT 3 Mind and Body

Page 46

- **Reading 1** Personality Revealed
- **Reading 2** Pets to the Rescue
- **Writing** The Example Essay | Using *such as*
- **Translation**
- **Weaving It Together**

UNIT 4 People Making a Difference

Page 68

- **Reading 1** Saving Africa's Largest Animals
- **Reading 2** Educating Kenya's Girls
- **Writing** The Descriptive Essay | The Narrative Essay
- **Translation**
- **Weaving It Together**

UNIT 5 Food

Page 92

- **Reading 1** Sushi Crosses the Pacific
- **Reading 2** What's for Breakfast?
- **Writing** Comparison and Contrast Words and Phrases | Using *while* and *whereas* | Using *although*, *even though*, and *though*
- **Translation**
- **Weaving It Together**

UNIT 6 Language

Page 114

- **Reading 1** Keeping It Secret
- **Reading 2** English Around the World
- **Writing** Writing about Reasons | Introducing Reasons with *because* and *as* | Words That Signal Cause and Effect | Using *therefore* and *consequently*
- **Translation**
- **Weaving It Together**

UNIT 7 Environment

Page 138

- **Reading 1** Behind Bars at the Zoo
- **Reading 2** Crops, Codes, and Controversy
- **Writing** Relevant Support | Using Factual Details to Support Your Opinion
- **Translation**
- **Weaving It Together**

UNIT 8 Readings from Literature

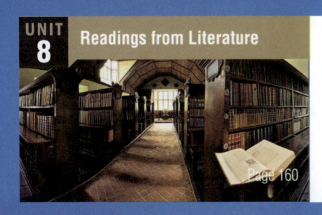

Page 160

- **Reading 1** The Road Not Taken
- **Reading 2** The Story of the Mouse Merchant
- **Writing** Imagery | Writing an Analysis of a Poem | Personal Narrative
- **Translation**
- **Weaving It Together**

UNIT 1

Symbols

The 15th-century Prague Astronomical Clock in Prague, Czech Republic

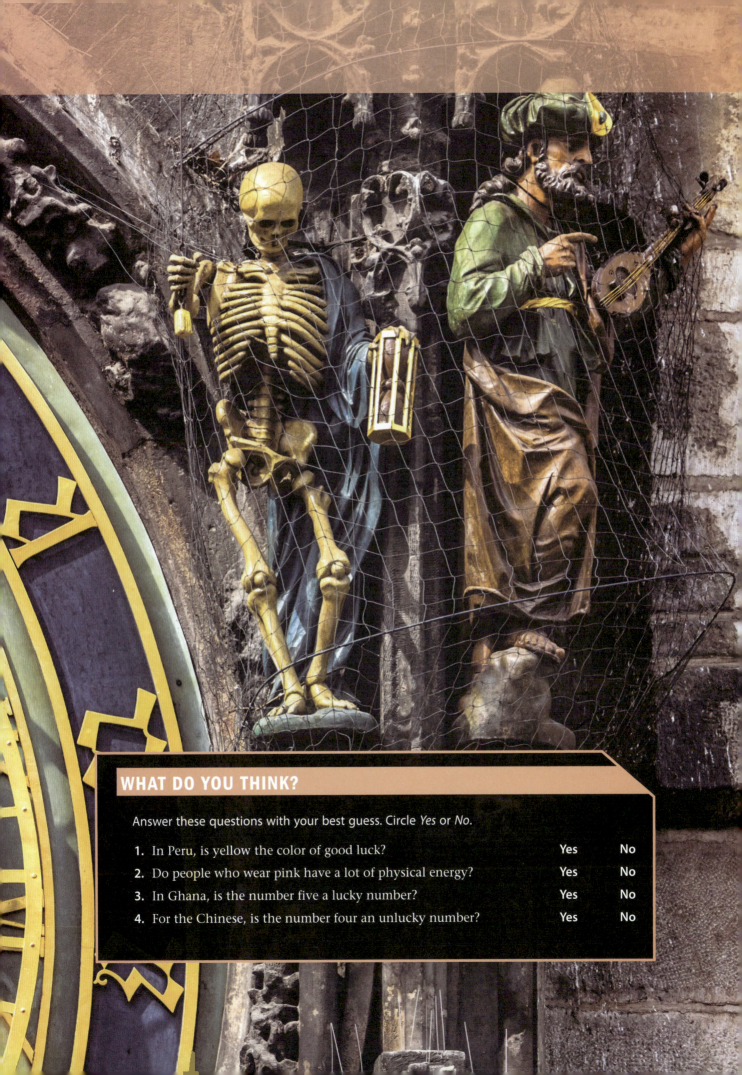

WHAT DO YOU THINK?

Answer these questions with your best guess. Circle *Yes* or *No*.

1. In Peru, is yellow the color of good luck? Yes No
2. Do people who wear pink have a lot of physical energy? Yes No
3. In Ghana, is the number five a lucky number? Yes No
4. For the Chinese, is the number four an unlucky number? Yes No

Reading 1

Pre-Reading

Preparing for the Reading Topic

A Discuss these questions with your classmates.

1. What do you think of the color of the house in the photo? Would you like to live in this house? What color do you think is a good color to paint the outside of a house?

2. Look at the color of the walls of the room you are in now. Do you think the color of the walls affects how you feel? In what way?

3. Imagine that the walls of the room were all red or all black. How do you think that would affect how you feel?

B What feelings do you associate with each of the following colors? Match each color with a feeling. Then after you have read "Color Me Pink", review your answers.

_____ 1. blue   a. energy

_____ 2. red   b. contentment

_____ 3. green   c. wealth

_____ 4. yellow   d. courage

_____ 5. brown   e. sadness

_____ 6. pink   f. peace

Key Vocabulary

As you read "Color Me Pink", pay attention to the following words and see if you can work out their meanings from the context.

sensitive	pace
soothe	attitude
select	stimulating
subconsciously	coincidence
contentment	ailments

A house known as "The Pink Palace", located near Stockholm, Sweden

Color Me Pink

1. Red, white, pink, purple—what is your favorite color? We are all **sensitive** to color. There are some colors we like a lot and some we don't like at all. Some colors **soothe** us, others excite us, some make us happy, and others make us sad. People are affected by color more than they realize because color is tied to all aspects of our lives.

2. Experts in colorgenics, the study of the language of color, believe that the colors we wear say a lot about us. Do you know why you **select** a shirt or dress of a certain color when you look through your clothes in the morning? Colorgenics experts say that we **subconsciously** choose to wear certain colors in order to communicate our desires, emotions, and needs.

3. Colorgenics experts claim that the colors of our clothes send messages to others

about our mood, personality, and desires. For these experts, pink expresses the peace and **contentment** of the wearer and awakens love and kindness. People who often wear pink are supposed to be warm and understanding. The message is that you would like to share your peace and happiness with others. Red garments, on the other hand, indicate a high level of physical energy. People who wear red like to live life at a fast **pace**. Brown is the color of wealth, and it shows a need for independence. Wearers of green have a love of nature and enjoy peaceful moments. They often like to be left alone with their thoughts.

4   Although colorgenics may be a recent area of study, associating colors with emotions is not new. Colors have always been used in phrases to describe not only our feelings, but also our physical health and attitudes. Red with rage describes anger; in the pink means to be in good health; feeling blue is a sad way to feel; and green with envy indicates a jealous **attitude**.

5   Color is used symbolically in all cultures, and it plays an important role in ceremonies and festivities. Yellow is a symbol of luck in Peru[1], and it can be seen just about everywhere during New Year's celebrations—in flowers, clothing, and decorations. Some Peruvians[2] say, "The more yellow you have around you, the luckier you will be in the new year." Yellow is also an important color to the Vietnamese[3], who use it at weddings and also on their flag, where it represents courage, victory, and sacrifice. In many cultures, white symbolizes purity, which is why brides often wear white wedding gowns. Black, on the other hand, symbolizes death, and it is often the color people wear to funerals.

6   Colorgenics experts also say that colors are not only a mirror of ourselves, but they have an effect on us as well. Blue is calming, while red is **stimulating** and exciting. It's no **coincidence** that racing cars are often painted red. Yellow is a happy color that makes us feel good about life. Pink awakens love and kindness.

7   Some experts are so convinced that colors have a strong effect on us that they believe colors can be used to heal. They say that by concentrating our thoughts on certain colors, we can cause energy to go to the parts of the body that need treatment. White light is said to be cleansing, and it can balance the body's entire system. Yellow stimulates the mind and creates a positive attitude, so it can help against depression. Green, which has a calming and restful effect, is supposed to be good for heart conditions. Books are now available that teach people how to heal with color. These books provide long lists of **ailments** and the colors that can heal them.

8   Some psychologists and physicians also use color to help them treat patients with emotional and psychological problems. By giving patients what is called the Lüscher Color Test, in which they select the colors they like and dislike, doctors can learn many things about patients' personalities.

9   In conclusion, the study of color can help us to understand ourselves and to improve our lives. It offers an alternative way to heal the body and spirit, and it can help us understand what others are trying to communicate. We can then respond to their needs and achieve a new level of understanding.

---

1 Peru 秘鲁
2 Peruvian 秘鲁人
3 Vietnamese 越南人

Vocabulary

Vocabulary in Context

A Complete these sentences with the words in the box.

ailments	coincidence	pace	sensitive	stimulating
attitude	contentment	select	soothe	subconsciously

1. People who are sick have _____.
2. To _____ someone is to comfort the person and make the person feel better.
3. Something that excites us and makes us active is _____.
4. To do something _____ is to act without actively knowing that you are doing it.
5. When things happen by _____, they appear to be connected in some way but really are not.
6. Your _____ is the feeling or emotion you have toward something.
7. A state of happiness and satisfaction is _____.
8. _____ is the speed at which we do things.
9. People who are able to understand other people's feelings and problems are _____.
10. To _____ is to choose something or someone.

B Answer these questions with complete sentences.

1. What color **soothes** you?

2. What color do you find **stimulating**?

3. Do you read English at a slow, medium, or fast **pace**?

4. What is an **ailment** many people have some time in their life?

5. What color do you usually **select** for your clothes?

C Now write your own sentences. Use the following words in the sentences: **attitude**, **coincidence**, **contentment**, **sensitive**, and **subconsciously**.

_____
_____
_____
_____
_____

Vocabulary Building

Complete these sentences with the correct form of the **bold** words. You may use your dictionary. The first one is done for you.

1. **contentment**
    a. My father is _____content_____ to sit at home and watch TV every night.
    b. After I finish all my work, I get a feeling of _____.

2. **select**
    a. I always _____ soothing colors for my bedroom.
    b. The salesperson showed me a _____ of colors to choose from.

3. **stimulating**
    a. Some people find listening to music _____ while they work.
    b. The interesting lecture provided him with the _____ to write his paper.

Reading Comprehension

A Circle the letter of the best answer.

1. Which of the following best expresses the main idea of this passage?
    a. Learning about colors can help us to express our ideas more clearly.
    b. Learning about colors can help us to control our desires.
    c. Learning about colors can help us to understand ourselves and others.
    d. Learning about colors can help us to feel happier.

2. Which of the following is true about colors?
    a. Colors can change our lives.
    b. Many aspects in our lives are connected with colors.
    c. A certain color symbolizes the same thing in all cultures.
    d. Color is the most important way for human communication.

3. What function does color NOT perform in clothing?
    a. It can indicate the wearer's personality.
    b. It can indicate the wearer's desire.

c. It can indicate the wearer's feelings.

d. It can indicate the wearer's ability.

4. Which statement is NOT true according to the text?

   a. Yellow makes people sad in some cultures.

   b. Yellow is eye-catching as compared with other colors.

   c. Yellow is used as a cure for people with psychological problems.

   d. Yellow is associated with luck in some cultures.

5. What's the purpose of the Lüscher Color Test?

   a. To communicate with patients.

   b. To cure patients' psychological troubles.

   c. To find out patients' personality.

   d. To discover what color most people like.

B Each statement below contains information given in the passage. Identify the paragraph from which the information is derived.

1. Some experts believe that colors can be used to heal.   Paragraph _____
2. Colors are often used in a symbolic way in all cultures.   Paragraph _____
3. Colors say something about our mood, personality and desires.   Paragraph _____
4. Doctors can learn about patients' personalities by using colors.   Paragraph _____
5. The idea that colors are associated with our emotions is not new.   Paragraph _____
6. Colors not only reflect our personalities but also have an effect on us.   Paragraph _____

Critical Thinking

Discuss these questions with your classmates.

1. What colors are you wearing today? Do you think they are a reflection of your feelings?

2. Look at the colors your classmates are wearing. Do you think the colors they are wearing match their personalities?

3. What colors are symbolic in your culture? What are they symbolic of?

4. What do you like or dislike about the way colors are used in your environment—for example, the colors in your school or classroom?

5. How would you change the colors in your school or classroom?

Reading 2

Pre-Reading

Preparing for the Reading Topic

A Discuss these questions with your classmates.

1. What is your lucky number?
2. In which cultures are the following numbers lucky or unlucky: 4, 7, and 13?
3. How superstitious are you?

B What nationalities or cultures regard these numbers as important or lucky? Match each number with a nationality or culture. Then after you have read "And the Lucky Number Is...", review your answers.

_____ 1. Chinese   a. 13
_____ 2. Egyptian   b. 5
_____ 3. British and French   c. 3
_____ 4. Ancient Babylonians d. 4

Key Vocabulary

As you read "And the Lucky Number Is...", pay attention to the following words and see if you can work out their meanings from the context.

superstitions	omen
considered	enterprise
endurance	assign
reputation	omitted
misfortune	persisted

A Pythagoras tree shows the beauty and mystery of mathematics. Using Pythagoras's Theorem, squares fit together to form right-angled triangles.

And the Lucky Number Is…

1   Do you believe that seven is a lucky number or that bad luck happens in sets of three? If so, your ideas are as old as Pythagoras[1], a Greek philosopher who lived 2,600 years ago. Pythagoras believed that certain numbers and their multiples had mystical power. For centuries, people have given importance to numbers and developed **superstitions** about them. Many of these superstitions have been passed on through the generations and still exist today.

2   Many of the superstitions surrounding numbers have a basis in science and nature. For example, early astrologers believed that seven planets governed the universe and therefore the lives of human beings. A seventh child was thought to have special gifts. Human life was divided into seven ages. Every seventh year was believed to bring great change. If a person's date of birth could be divided by seven, that person's life would

---

1 Pythagoras 毕达哥拉斯，古希腊哲学家、数学家

be lucky. For the ancient Babylonians[2], three was a lucky number because it symbolized birth, life, and death. Some people still believe that a dream repeated three times comes true.

3   Numbers don't have the same meaning in all cultures. Five is **considered** a most holy and lucky number in Egypt. But in Ghana[3], the Ashanti[4] people consider five to be an unlucky number. To give someone five of anything is to wish the person evil. The ancient Greeks and Egyptians thought the number four was a perfect number symbolizing unity, **endurance**, and balance. However, the Chinese consider the number four to be unlucky because it sounds like the word for death.

4   The number that seems to be almost universally considered unlucky is 13. No other number has had such a bad **reputation** for so long. The ancient Romans regarded it as a symbol of death, destruction, and **misfortune**. One of the earliest written stories about the number 13 appears in Norwegian[5] mythology. This story tells about a feast at Valhalla[6] to which 12 gods were invited. Loki[7], the god of evil, came uninvited, raising the number to 13. In the struggle to throw out Loki, Balder[8], the favorite of the gods, was killed.

5   There are many superstitions regarding the number 13. For example, in Britain it's considered a bad **omen** for 13 people to sit at a table. Some say that the person who rises first at this table will meet with misfortune, even death, within a year. Others say it's the last person to rise. Some British people think it's unlucky to have 13 people in a room, especially for the person closest to the door. The thirteenth day of the month isn't considered a good day on which to begin any new **enterprise**, including marriage, or to set out on a journey. Many people believe that Friday the thirteenth is the unluckiest day in the year. This belief is so widespread that there are horror movies called *Friday the Thirteenth*.

6   Some people will go to great lengths to avoid the number 13. Hotel owners do not usually **assign** the number 13 to a room, preferring to label it 12A or 14 instead. The French never issue the house address 13, while in Italy the number 13 is **omitted** from the national lottery. Some airlines have no thirteenth row on their planes, and office and apartment buildings rarely have a thirteenth floor.

7   From ancient civilizations to modern societies, the belief in the magic of numbers has **persisted** in spite of the advances in science and technology. There is nothing quite as stubborn as superstition. Even today, in the twenty-first century, people still believe in bad luck and omens. In the future, people may work in space stations or travel the universe in starships, but there probably won't be a "Starbase 13" or a rocket liftoff on Friday the thirteenth. A seventh voyage will be a good one, and the third time around will still be lucky.

---

2 Babylonian 巴比伦人
3 Ghana 加纳，非洲西部国家
4 Ashanti 非洲西部阿善堤地区的人
5 Norwegian 挪威的
6 Valhalla 瓦尔哈拉殿堂，北欧神话中死亡之神奥丁款待阵亡将士英灵的殿堂
7 Loki 洛基，北欧神话里的火神
8 Balder 巴尔德，北欧神话中以美丽和善闻名的神

Vocabulary

A What are the meanings of the **bold** words? Circle the letter of the best answer.

1. For centuries people have had **superstitions** about numbers.
   - a. silly fears
   - b. unreliable beliefs
   - c. exciting legends
   - d. old traditions

2. In some countries the number five is **considered** lucky; in others it is not.
   - a. designed
   - b. formed
   - c. believed
   - d. placed

3. Four was considered by ancient Egyptians to be a perfect number symbolizing unity, **endurance**, and balance.
   - a. continuation
   - b. equality
   - c. independence
   - d. strength

4. The number 13 has had a bad **reputation**.
   - a. grade
   - b. direction
   - c. condition
   - d. name

5. The Romans regarded 13 as a symbol of death, destruction, and **misfortune**.
   - a. bad luck
   - b. opportunity
   - c. injury
   - d. unhappiness

6. It's considered a bad **omen** for 13 people to sit at a table.
   - a. promise
   - b. sign
   - c. action
   - d. event

7. The thirteenth is not considered a good day on which to begin any new **enterprise**.
   - a. building
   - b. project
   - c. journey
   - d. meeting

8. Hotel owners will not usually **assign** the number 13 to a room.
   - a. transfer
   - b. choose
   - c. allow
   - d. give

9. In Italy, the number 13 is **omitted** from the lottery.
   - a. left out
   - b. added
   - c. repeated
   - d. replaced

10. The belief in the magic of numbers has **persisted**.
    - a. gone away
    - b. become greater
    - c. changed
    - d. continued

B Answer these questions with complete sentences.

1. What sport do you need **endurance** for?
   _____

2. What schools have a good **reputation**?
   _____

3. What vegetable is **considered** to be healthy for you?
   _____

4. What information cannot be **omitted** when you fill out forms?
   _____

5. What does your teacher usually **assign** for homework?
   _____

C Now write your own sentences. Use the following words in the sentences: **superstitions**, **persisted**, **misfortune**, **enterprise**, and **omen**.

_____
_____
_____
_____

Reading Comprehension

A Circle the letter of the best answer.

1. Which of the following best expresses the main purpose of this passage?
   a. To highlight the foolishness of superstition and urge the readers not to believe in them.
   b. To explain the magical power of numbers.
   c. To explain the meaning of numbers in different cultures.
   d. To introduce long-standing superstitions about numbers.

2. Throughout the ages, people have _____.
   a. written stories about numbers
   b. given meaning and importance to numbers
   c. considered five a lucky number
   d. used numbers to tell the future

3. The earliest written stories about the number 13 appeared in _____ mythology.
   a. Greek   b. Roman
   c. Norwegian   d. Egyptian

4. Which is NOT true about numbers?

   a. To the Babylonians, three was a lucky number.

   b. Five is considered a lucky number for the Ashanti people.

   c. For the ancient Greeks, four was a perfect number.

   d. The thirteenth day in a month is considered unlucky for marriage.

5. In ancient history, every _____ year was believed to bring change in a person's life.

   a. third

   b. seventh

   c. fourth

   d. fifth

B Do the following statements reflect the views of the writer in the passage? Write:

YES if the statement reflects the views of the writer;

NO if the statement contradicts the views of the writer;

NG (not given) if there is no information about this in the passage.

_____ 1. In ancient times, people thought the seventh child had special gifts.

_____ 2. Interpreters of dreams believe that a dream repeated three times is bad luck.

_____ 3. In ancient history, every third year was believed to bring change in a person's life.

_____ 4. To the Babylonians, three was a lucky number.

_____ 5. Five is considered a lucky number for the Ashanti people.

_____ 6. For the ancient Greeks, four was a perfect number.

Critical Thinking

Discuss these questions with your classmates.

1. What superstitions are there in China?

2. What are the lucky and unlucky numbers in China?

3. Describe an object used as a symbol. Where and how is it used?

4. Why do you think some people give importance to the astrological sign under which they were born?

5. Some people say they can foretell the future by looking at cards, coffee grounds, tea leaves, and so on. How do you think?

Writing

Writing Skills

Paragraph Structure

A *paragraph* is a basic unit of organization for writing a group of sentences that develop one main idea. There are three parts in a paragraph: a *topic sentence*, *supporting sentences*, and a *concluding sentence*.

- The **topic sentence** is the most important sentence in the paragraph. It is the main idea of the paragraph. The topic sentence controls and limits the ideas that can be discussed in a paragraph. The topic sentence has two parts: the *topic* and the *controlling idea*.

- The **topic** is the subject of the paragraph.

    EXAMPLE: <u>The color yellow</u> is the color of mental activity.
                     topic

- The **controlling idea** limits or controls your topic to one aspect that you want to write about.

    EXAMPLE: <u>The color brown</u> shows <u>a desire for stability</u>.
                 topic   controlling idea

- A topic can have more than one controlling idea. For example, you could write one paragraph about the color brown indicating the desire for stability and another paragraph about the color brown indicating wealth.

- **Supporting sentences** develop the topic sentence. They give the reader reasons, examples, and more facts about the topic sentence. They must all be related to the topic sentence.

- The last sentence of your paragraph is called the concluding sentence. This sentence signals the end of the paragraph.

- The **concluding sentence** is similar to the topic sentence. Both are general sentences. The concluding sentence can be written in two ways: You can state the topic sentence in different words, or you can summarize the main points in the paragraph.

- Begin a concluding sentence with the phrases *In conclusion* or *In summary*.

Exercise 1

Circle the topic and underline the controlling idea in each of these topic sentences.

1. The colors we wear change our emotions.
2. People who wear orange like to communicate with others.
3. People who wear red clothes want to have fun.
4. Shoes give us lots of information about the person wearing them.
5. Patterns on clothing give us clues to the mood of the wearer.
6. People who wear yellow are often creative.
7. Turquoise is good for people who have decisions to make.
8. People who wear green often like the outdoors.

Exercise 2

Look at the underlined topic sentences. In each case, one of the sentences below does not support the topic sentence. Circle the letter of the sentence that does not support the topic.

1. Colors are often divided into two groups, warm and cold.
   a. The warm colors are red, pink, yellow, and orange.
   b. These colors are associated with activity and energy.
   c. Violet is the color of royalty and is often worn by political and religious leaders.
   d. The cold colors—blue, purple, violet, and brown—are calm and mysterious.

2. Socks give us clues to a person's inner personality.
   a. Socks are available in more colors now than ever before.
   b. Red socks show that the wearer has lots of energy that he or she needs to release.
   c. Wearers of white socks are often hiding their true feelings.
   d. Green socks are worn when a person feels the need for rest and relaxation.

3. Colors are symbolic and have many different meanings to people around the world.
   a. In America, red, white, and blue—the colors of the flag—symbolize patriotism.
   b. Green is a sign of birth and new life to the Irish.
   c. Blue looks good on people with blue eyes.
   d. Some colors, such as pink and blue, represent female and male.

Exercise 3

Write a topic sentence and a concluding sentence for each of these paragraphs.

1. **Topic sentence:** _____

   If your favorite color is white, you are probably very moral and sometimes have old-fashioned ideas about romance. People who like red, on the other hand, want excitement, variety, and change and are often more interested in passion than true love. Pink lovers are warm and understanding people who believe in loyalty and make good mates. Those who like the color blue are emotional and romantic and need lots of attention from their partners.

   Concluding sentence: _____

2. **Topic sentence:** _____

   Violet is a color that affects the bones in the body and can be used to heal the pain of arthritis. Gold helps awaken a body's own healing energy. Blue clears the mind, and aqua is cooling and can ease a fever.

   Concluding sentence: _____

The Parts of an Essay

An *essay* is a piece of writing that is several paragraphs long. An essay, just like a paragraph, is about one topic. Since its topic is broad, the essay is divided into paragraphs, one for each major point.

- Look at the following diagram of an essay. Notice how the parts of an essay correspond to the parts of a paragraph.

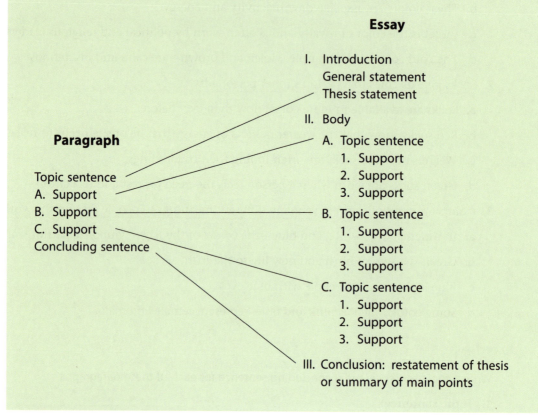

The Thesis Statement

An essay is controlled by one main idea. This main idea is called the *thesis statement*. The thesis statement is similar to the topic sentence in a paragraph, but it is broader and gives the controlling idea for the whole essay. The topic sentence in each of the body paragraphs of an essay should relate to the thesis statement.

- The thesis statement should be a complete sentence.

- The thesis statement should express an opinion, an idea, or a belief. It should be something that you can argue about. It should not be a plain fact.

    EXAMPLE: ***Fact:*** Water consists of hydrogen and oxygen.

    Thesis statement: The water in our homes may contain harmful chemicals.

- The thesis statement should not be a detail or an example.

    EXAMPLE: ***Detail or Example:*** In Hong Kong, the number eight is lucky.

    Thesis statement: There are many superstitions about even numbers around the world.

- The thesis statement may state or list how it will support an opinion.

    EXAMPLE: ***Thesis statement:*** Television has a bad influence on children for three main reasons.

Exercise 4

Read the following sentences. Some are thesis statements and some are details. Check (✓) the thesis statements.

_____ 1. People have always been superstitious about cats.
_____ 2. In certain parts of Asia, people believed that they became cats after they died.
_____ 3. There are many superstitions that are similar in several countries around the world.
_____ 4. It is said that to knock over the salt on a table is to meet trouble.

Exercise 5

Read the following essay written by a student. Then answer the questions at the end of the essay.

Superstitions in My Country

In the Middle East, especially Syria where I come from, people believe in some superstitions. Some of these superstitions are so strong that they are almost customs. These superstitions are about protecting against evil and bringing good luck. Two of the most popular superstitions are concerned with the evil eye and throwing water.

People believe that they must protect themselves from the evil eye of another person by putting turquoise beads in various places. A blue bead is pinned on newly born babies because babies are more vulnerable to an evil spirit and must be protected. Since houses must be protected, too, a blue bead, usually with a horseshoe, is placed near the doorway for protection against someone with an evil eye. Also, if people have an item of special value like a car or sewing machine, they must protect it with a blue bead.

Another popular superstition is throwing water, which is done at various times. When someone leaves on a trip, people throw water out of the window to wish the traveler a good trip. This is so the person will go and come back like water. Water is also thrown by people when a funeral procession goes by in the street, so that death will not come into the people's homes. The Armenians, who are Christians living in Syria, throw water on each other on a special Saint's Day in mid-July for fertility and prosperity.

In conclusion, certain superstitions have become rituals with the purpose of protecting and bringing good luck. Because people always want to be protected and have good luck, these age-old superstitions are as strong today as they were ages ago and probably will continue in the future.

1. What is the thesis statement for the whole essay? Where is it located? Circle it.
2. What are the topic sentences in each of the body paragraphs? Underline them.
3. Do each of the body paragraphs have supporting sentences?
4. Where is the concluding sentence? Is it a restatement of the thesis or a summary of the main points?

Writing Practice

Write Body Paragraphs

Choose one of the following topics to write two body paragraphs of an essay.

1. Superstitions that bring good luck and superstitions that bring bad luck
2. People avoiding the evil eye of someone both in their homes and outside
3. Superstitions about New Year's Day and weddings

Pre-Write

A Work with a partner and brainstorm examples for your topic.

B Make a list of your examples, and work on topic sentences for two body paragraphs.

Outline

Fill in the outline below. Write your topic sentence for each body paragraph, and pick the three best examples from Exercise B in Pre-Write for each body paragraph. Use these examples as your supporting details. Finally, write your concluding sentence.

Paragraph Outline

Body Paragraph 1

Topic sentence: _____

_____

   Supporting detail 1: _____

   Supporting detail 2: _____

   Supporting detail 3: _____

Concluding sentence: _____

_____

Body Paragraph 2

Topic sentence: _____

_____

   Supporting detail 1: _____

   Supporting detail 2: _____

   Supporting detail 3: _____

Concluding sentence: _____

_____

Write and Revise Your Paragraphs

Translation

A Translate the following passage into English.

香囊（scented sachet），古代也称"香袋"，通常是用布缝制或彩色丝线编织的袋子，里面塞满香草（aromatic herbs）。香囊最初用来吸汗、驱虫和避邪，后来也用作装饰品。它们通常配有精致的图案，每个图案都象征着特别的含义。例如，双鱼或成对蝴蝶图案象征男女之爱；莲花或牡丹花（peony flower）等图案象征女性；松树和仙鹤图案象征长寿；石榴（guava）图案象征多子。

B Translate the following passage into Chinese.

When offering a gift, you should consider how to do it in a proper way. In China, gifts are usually packaged in red or other festive colors. White and black are not suitable in the packaging. When you offer a gift, the recipient may refuse to accept it at first for shyness, but finally he/she will accept it. Usually, the recipient won't open the gift until the guest leaves. In addition, there are some taboos in giving gifts. For example, it is inappropriate to present an umbrella as a gift to a couple because the word "umbrella" has the same pronunciation as the word "separate" in Chinese.

Weaving It Together

Unit Project

In this part, you are required to do some research among your classmates, friends or relatives. Collect information about colors. Then give a presentation to your classmates. The following questions can be used as references.

1. How do the colors you are wearing make you feel?
2. How do colors affect your appetite?
3. What colors in your surroundings increase or reduce your appetite?
4. Do colors always reflect your feelings or personality?
5. What is your favorite color? How do you use that color in daily life?

Searching the Internet

A Search the Internet for information about "animals and color". Find answers to these questions:

1. Which animals see in color? And what colors do they see?
2. Do birds and insects see colors?
3. What is your opinion of the sites you visited? Do you believe the information they contain? Why or why not?

B Search the Internet for interesting facts about numerology. Share the information with your classmates.

What Do You Think Now?

Refer to Page 3 at the beginning of this unit. Do you know the answers now? Complete the sentence, or circle the best answer.

1. In Peru, the color for good luck is _____.
2. People who wear pink (have/do not have) a lot of physical energy.
3. In Ghana, the number five is (a lucky/an unlucky) number.
4. For the Chinese, the number _____ is unlucky.

Broadening Your Horizon

Color Symbolism in Chinese Culture

Color symbolism in Chinese culture differs from the Western one in many respects.

In general, red is the color of honesty and virtue, associated with good manners (fire, summer, south, happiness and fortune). Yellow is the gods' color (glory and prosperity), associated with center, earth, the season between spring and summer, law and order, loyalty and faith. Green is associated with east, spring, goodness, life and inner peace; many goddesses choose green as the color of their garb; and in dramas or operas, demons and devils have green faces. Blue is associated with sky, sea, desire for knowledge and a promise of great achievement or prominent status. Black is associated with north, winter, water, dark but also wisdom and honor; and in theaters, a face painted black signifies an honest, sincere man. White is associated with woe, autumn, sunset, and old age; and in theaters, a white face signifies a scheming or deceiving character.

B

Your Personality Color

To discover your personality color, ask yourself: What is my favorite color?

Answer this question now before reading any further.

Don't think about it, be spontaneous with your answer; accept the first color that comes into your mind and don't analyze your choice.

It is this instinctive choice of a color that tells you a lot about yourself, such as how you function and how others see you.

It is the means to understand your behavior and your character traits as well as your physical, mental, emotional and spiritual states.

It reflects the way you operate in the world, your strengths and weaknesses, your vulnerabilities, your deepest needs and your challenges at that time in your life.

C

Lucky Number 4

People whose lucky number is four are usually endowed with excellent management capability. They are good at summarizing various documents, making complicated situations simple and clearly handling problems. Since most of these people also lack a sense of security, they pursue steady relationships to make themselves feel protected. Besides, these people often fear or hate changes in life and they are the most stubborn compared with people having other lucky numbers. Though they may have realized their own weaknesses, they hardly want to change. What's more, they argue well and are hard to influence when they take an opposing view.

UNIT 2
Customs

Hanging on a tree outside a shrine in Japan are omikuji papers. It is a custom for people to buy them to read inside and learn about their future.

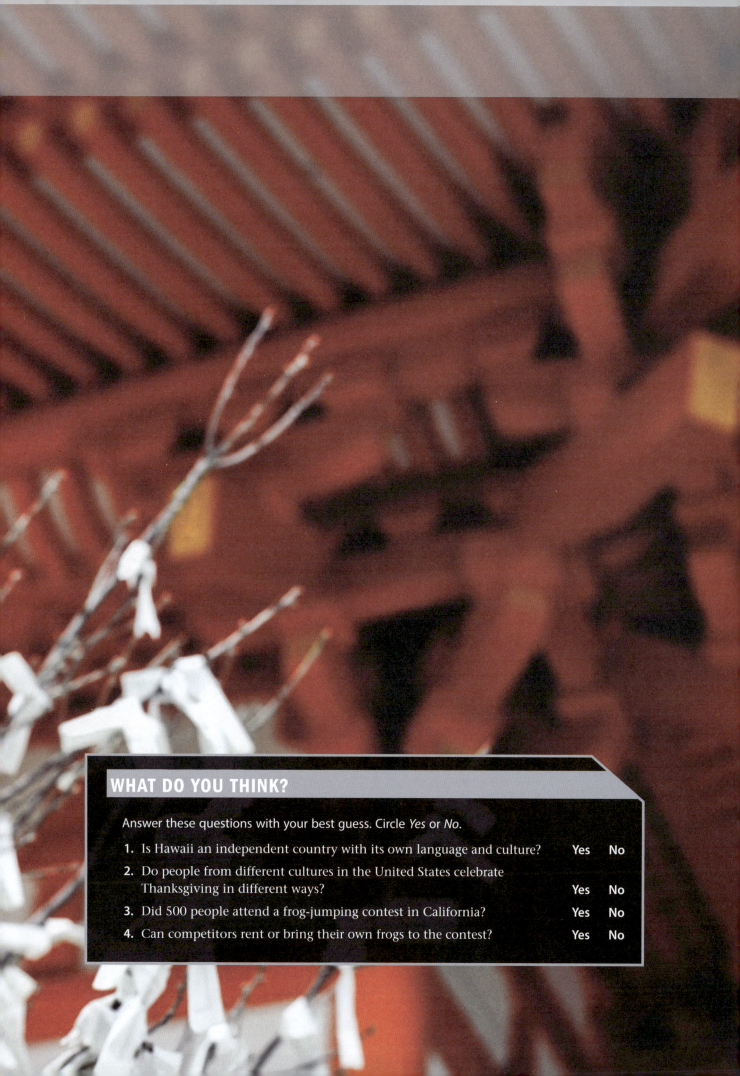

WHAT DO YOU THINK?

Answer these questions with your best guess. Circle *Yes* or *No*.

1. Is Hawaii an independent country with its own language and culture? Yes No
2. Do people from different cultures in the United States celebrate Thanksgiving in different ways? Yes No
3. Did 500 people attend a frog-jumping contest in California? Yes No
4. Can competitors rent or bring their own frogs to the contest? Yes No

Reading ▪ 1

Pre-Reading

Preparing for the Reading Topic

A Discuss these questions with your classmates.

1. What do you know about Hawaii?

2. What do you know about the U.S. holiday—Thanksgiving?

3. What do you think is happening in the photo on Page 28?

B Can you guess the meanings of these Hawaiian words? Write down your guesses. Then after you have read "Thanksgiving—Hawaiian Style", review your answers.

1. Hawaiians celebrate the Fourth of July with a big *luau* for all of their friends and family.

    luau: _____

2. They often wear colorful *muumuus* at celebrations.

    muumuus: _____

3. Around their necks, they wear *leis*.

    leis: _____

4. The pig is roasted in an *imu*.

    imu: _____

Key Vocabulary

As you read "Thanksgiving—Hawaiian Style", pay attention to the following words and phrases and see if you can work out their meanings from the context.

diversity	bundles
paste	shovel
exploding	pat down
line	trace
pile up	emerge

Hawaiian dancers perform in Honolulu, Hawaii, U.S.A.

Thanksgiving– Hawaiian Style

1. Fireworks. Hot dogs. Bands marching down Main Street. These are the pictures that come to many people's minds when they think of U.S. holidays. But the United States is a vast country made up of people from many different cultures, and the celebration of holidays reflects this **diversity**.

2. In the Chinatown section of San Francisco, rice and snow peas are a part of many holiday meals. In New Mexico[1], one might encounter chili peppers, *piñatas*[2], and Mexican music on the Fourth of July. In Hawaii, one popular way to celebrate a holiday

---

[1] New Mexico 新墨西哥州，美国州名
[2] *piñatas* （西班牙）彩罐

is with a feast, or *luau*, which has been a Hawaiian tradition for centuries.

3   Hawaii is the only state in the United States that was once an independent country with its own language and culture. Today, many Hawaiians continue to celebrate traditional Hawaiian holidays, such as Prince Kuhio Day[3], Kamehameha Day[4], and Aloha Week[5]. In celebration of their Hawaiian ancestry, Islanders might dress in traditional clothes such as loose dresses called *muumuus* or colorful shirts. Around their necks they might wear *leis*, or rings of flowers.

4   Even when it comes to celebrating a traditional American holiday, such as Thanksgiving, Hawaiians give it their own special flavor. They might place pumpkins on doorsteps and **paste** cardboard pilgrims[6] on windows, but chances are good there will also be a turkey or a pig roasting under the ground in an earth oven, or *imu*.

5   Cooking in an *imu* is an ancient Islands' custom that requires much work and cooperation among family members. Preparations begin several days before Thanksgiving, when the family goes down to the beach or to the mouth of a stream to fill bags with smooth, rounded lava stones. They choose the stones carefully for their shape and size and for holes that will prevent the rocks from **exploding** when they are heated.

6   To prepare the *imu*, the men first dig a large hole in the shape of a bowl about three feet (0.91 meters) wide and two feet (0.61 meters) deep. They then **line** the bottom and sides of the hole with the lava rocks. They cut up firewood and **pile** it **up**, ready for the holiday morning when a fire is lit inside the hole. As the fire gets bigger and hotter, more rocks are placed in the hole. Finally, the lava rocks get so hot that they glow red and white. The fire is then brushed aside, and several of the hot rocks are placed inside the turkey or pig. The meat is then wrapped in the long, broad leaves of the *ti* plant and tied up tightly with wire.

---

3 Prince Kuhio Day 库希奥王子纪念日，每年的3月26日
4 Kamehameha Day 卡美哈美哈国王日，在每年的6月份举行
5 Aloha Week 阿罗哈节，在每年的9月份举行
6 pilgrims 1620年移居美洲的英国清教徒

Cooks prepare food in an *imu* on Maui Island, Hawaii.

7   Before the pig or turkey is placed in the *imu*, the men spread chopped pieces of banana plant over the hot rocks. The white, juicy lining of this plant makes a lot of steam, but it can also cause a bitter taste, so *ti* leaves are layered over it. Finally, the pig or turkey is placed in the *imu*, along with sweet potatoes, pineapple, plantain[7], vegetables, and even fresh fish—all wrapped in *ti* leaves.

8   The men spread more hot rocks over the **bundles** of food, then more *ti* leaves, a layer of wet bags, and a canvas covering. They **shovel** dirt into the hole and **pat down** the dirt until it is smooth. Not a **trace** can be seen of either the meal or the earth oven in which it is cooking.

9   Three to four hours later, the dirt is shoveled away. The men dip their hands in cold water and then quickly remove the burned leaves and rocks, allowing delicious smells to **emerge** from the oven. The bundles of cooked food are taken out, uncovered, and placed on platters, ready for a different kind of Thanksgiving meal, cooked and served Hawaiian style.

Vocabulary

Vocabulary in Context

A Complete these sentences with the words or phrases in the box.

| bundles | emerge | line | pat down | shovel |
| diversity | exploding | paste | pile up | trace |

1. To _____ is to place a number of things on top of the other.
2. To stick something to something else is to _____ it.
3. A(n) _____ is a sign that something existed in a certain place.
4. To _____ something is to tap or hit it gently to flatten or smooth it.
5. To cover the inside of something is to _____ it.
6. To _____ is to come into view or notice.
7. When digging a hole in the ground, if you lift and throw the dirt with a special tool, you _____ it.
8. _____ are groups of things fastened or tied together.
9. _____ is when something is bursting suddenly and violently making a loud noise.
10. _____ is the state of being different from one another.

B Answer these questions with complete sentences.

1. What is something that you might see **exploding** in the sky?

   _____

---

7 plantain 车前草，香蕉之一种

2. What is something you can have **bundles** of?

   _____

3. What can you **pile up**?

   _____

4. What types of things do you **pat down**?

   _____

5. What is something you can **shovel**?

   _____

C Now write your own sentences. Use the following words in the sentences: *emerge*, *line*, *paste*, *trace*, and *diversity*.

   _____
   _____
   _____
   _____

Vocabulary Building

Complete these sentences with the correct form of the **bold** words. You may use your dictionary.

1. explode
   a. We could hear the _____ from miles away.
   b. A can of soda _____ in the refrigerator and made a mess.

2. diversity
   a. New York is home to people of _____ cultures.
   b. The South American continent shows a _____ of climates.

3. emerge
   a. A few minutes ago, baby birds _____ from the nest.
   b. Scientists were worried by the _____ of the new virus.

Reading Comprehension

A Circle the letter of the best answer.

1. Which of the following is NOT mentioned as a way of celebrating holidays in America?
   a. Having dumplings.   b. Enjoying snow peas.
   c. Appreciating Mexican music.   d. Holding a feast.

2. What accounts for the fact that Hawaiians dress in traditional clothes on holidays?
   a. To show beauty.   b. To show personality.
   c. To show uniqueness.   d. To show respect for ancestry.

3. In Hawaii, people celebrate Thanksgiving _____.

a. because it is a traditional Hawaiian holiday

b. at a time different from other states of America

c. in the same way as they celebrate other holidays

d. with some typical American ways and Hawaiian customs

4. Cooking in an earth oven _____.

   a. is a Pan-American custom   b. involves the men only

   c. needs preparing beforehand   d. can be done without lava rocks

5. Which of the following steps is NOT included in preparing a Hawaiian Thanksgiving meal?

   a. Placing pieces of banana plant over hot rocks.

   b. Putting the meat wrapped in bamboo leaves in an *imu*.

   c. Spreading hot rocks over bundles of food.

   d. Patting down the dirt shoveled into the hole.

B Each statement below contains information given in the passage. Identify the paragraph from which the information is derived.

1. When celebrating Thanksgiving Day, Hawaiians add their own special custom to the festival.   Paragraph _____

2. America is a large country composed with people from many diverse cultures.   Paragraph _____

3. Several hours later, a distinctive Thanksgiving meal is ready and served in a Hawaiian style.   Paragraph _____

4. The pig or turkey, some vegetables and fruits which are bundled in *ti* leaves are put in an *imu*.   Paragraph _____

5. Nowadays people in Hawaii continue to observe traditional holidays to commemorate their ancestry.   Paragraph _____

6. Cooking in an earth oven is a family work that requires mutual cooperation.   Paragraph _____

7. Men dig a big hole in the shape of a bowl about 0.91 meters wide and 0.61 meters deep to prepare an *imu*.   Paragraph _____

8. Hot rocks, *ti* leaves, wet bags and a canvas covering are put on top of the wrapped food.   Paragraph _____

Critical Thinking

Discuss these questions with your classmates.

1. What Chinese and western traditional festivals do you know?

2. Give an example of a very old tradition that is still practiced during Chinese festivals.

3. Describe a method of making a traditional Chinese festival food.

4. What culture do you most admire for its foods and cooking methods? Why?

5. Nowadays mass travel and communication leave few societies untouched by others. Do you think it is a positive or negative trend? Explain why.

Reading 2

Pre-Reading

Preparing for the Reading Topic

A Discuss these questions with your classmates.

1. What is happening in the photo?
2. What other events with animals do you know?
3. What do you think of training animals for performance?

B Which of the following words do you think relate to frogs? Circle them and say how you think they are connected to the topic. Then after you have read "Hop to It!", review your ideas.

jump	jockey	launching pad
race	scream	whistle

Key Vocabulary

As you read "Hop to It!", pay attention to the following words and see if you can work out their meanings from the context.

inspiration	frustrate
accommodate	unpredictable
modest	fundamentals
launching pad	auction
incite	consolation

A young competitor encourages his frog to jump during a frog-jumping competition in May 2014.

Hop to It!

1 "He's good enough for one thing, I should judge—he can outjump any frog in Calaveras County," said Smiley in Mark Twain's[1] famous short story, "The Celebrated Jumping Frog of Calaveras[2] County". This was the **inspiration** for the Calaveras County Jumping Frog Contest, which has taken place every year since 1928 in the village of Angels Camp in Calaveras County, California. The first year, 15,000 people attended this unusual event—more than the entire population of Calaveras County at the time. The following year, the crowd doubled; and by

---

1 Mark Twain 马克·吐温
2 Calaveras 卡拉维拉斯，美国加州地名

1931, the event was so popular that two additional jumping areas had to be added to **accommodate** entries from around the world. Today, more than 50,000 spectators attend this event and the frog entries number 1,000.

2 Although the Calaveras County Jumping Frog Contest has gained international attention, the majority of the competitors are still people from Calaveras County. Anyone who would like to enter goes to the registration table, fills out a form, and pays a **modest** entry fee. The fee includes the cost of renting a frog in case the person who enters the contest doesn't already own one. Many people who live in the area go out and catch their frogs the night before, so they are "fresh" and ready to go on the day of the contest.

3 After entering the contest, the competitors must decide who will be the "jockey". This is the person who places the frog on the **launching pad** and then encourages the frog to jump. The goals of the entrants and their "jockeys" are, first of all, to have fun; second, to win a prize; and third, to set a new world frog-jumping record.

4 The contest starts when the "jockey" positions his or her frog and then yells, screams, jumps up and down, puffs, blows, whistles, or does whatever else is necessary to **incite** the frog to jump. The one thing that is not allowed is to touch the frog. Each frog is given 15 seconds to jump three times. Once a frog has made its three jumps, an official measures the distance from the center of the pad to the spot where the frog landed on its third jump. Naturally, the winning frog is usually the one that jumped in the straightest line rather than zigzagged around. Some frogs **frustrate** their "jockeys" by jumping back toward the launching pad after a spectacular first or second jump.

5 Like any of nature's creations, frogs are **unpredictable**—that is, unless they had once been to Bill Steed's famous Croaker College. "Students" who went to the college in the past were given a 240-hour frog-training course to teach them the **fundamentals** of frog jumping under pressure. They worked out in a pool, lifted tiny weights, did chin-ups and high dives, ate centipede soup and ladybug salad, and generally prepared for the big day. Did graduates of Croaker College really win frog-jumping contests more often? That's a question Bill Steed prefers not to answer.

6 After the winners have been announced and the prizes given, the participants can take their frogs (or return their "rentals") and go home, or they can stay and enjoy the rest of the Calaveras County Fair. They can listen to country music, view craft displays, attend a horse race, watch a farm animal **auction**, and more. For those people who think nothing quite compares to the excitement of the jumping frogs, however, there is the **consolation** of knowing there is always next year.

Vocabulary

A What are the meanings of the **bold** words? Circle the letter of the best answer.

1. This is the **inspiration** for the Calaveras County Jumping Frog Contest.
   - a. influence
   - b. information
   - c. description
   - d. advertisement

2. Two jumping areas had to be added to **accommodate** the entries from around the world.
   - a. invite
   - b. announce
   - c. encourage
   - d. provide for

3. Anyone who would like to enter pays a **modest** entry fee.
   - a. small
   - b. expensive
   - c. formal
   - d. official

4. The "jockey" places the frog on the **launching pad**.
   - a. winner's circle
   - b. take-off point
   - c. measuring place
   - d. finish line

5. The "jockey" does whatever is necessary to **incite** the frog to jump.
   - a. excite
   - b. calm
   - c. demonstrate
   - d. frighten

6. Some frogs **frustrate** their "jockeys".
   - a. stop
   - b. satisfy
   - c. upset
   - d. reward

7. Frogs are **unpredictable**.
   - a. experienced
   - b. surprising
   - c. native
   - d. understandable

8. At Croaker College, frogs were taught the **fundamentals** of jumping.
   - a. possibilities
   - b. basics
   - c. origins
   - d. tricks

9. People can attend a farm animal **auction** at the fair.
   - a. show
   - b. contest
   - c. race
   - d. sale

10. There is the **consolation** of knowing there's always next year.
    - a. pressure
    - b. benefit
    - c. comfort
    - d. excitement

B Answer these questions with complete sentences.

1. What activity in your English class can **frustrate** you?

   _____
   _____

2. What simple tenses are the **fundamentals** of English grammar?

   _____
   _____

3. Which month has the most **unpredictable** weather in your city?

   _____
   _____

4. What can be sold in an **auction**?

5. Where do you pay a **modest** fee to enter?

C Now write your own sentences. Use the following words in the sentences: ***inspiration***, ***accommodate***, ***launching pad***, ***incite***, and ***consolation***.

Reading Comprehension

A Circle the letter of the best answer.

1. What do we learn about the Calaveras County Jumping Frog Contest?
    a. It is a common international event.
    b. It is a formal international event.
    c. It is an unusual but popular event.
    d. It is a popular but expensive event.

2. The Jumping Frog Contest _____.
    a. is open to everyone, even those without frogs
    b. is open only to competitors with "fresh" frogs
    c. is open only to graduates from Croaker College
    d. is open only to local people from Calaveras County

3. Which one of the following is NOT the purpose of holding the Contest?
    a. To entertain people.
    b. To get a prize.
    c. To learn about frogs.
    d. To break a record.

4. What do we know about Croaker College?
    a. It aims at improving people's physical health.
    b. It aims at relieving people's mental pressure.
    c. It aims at prolonging frogs' lifespan.
    d. It aims at training frogs' jumping ability.

5. Which of the following best expresses the main idea of the passage?

   a. Advertising Calaveras County frogs.

   b. Listing some ways to win the Contest.

   c. Describing the process of the Contest.

   d. Encouraging more people to join in the Contest.

B Answer the questions below using NO MORE THAN THREE WORDS from the passage.

1. Which contest has taken place every year since 1928 in the village of Angels Camp in Calaveras County?

   _____

2. Who places the frog on the launching pad?

   _____

3. How long is allowed for each frog to jump three times in the contest?

   _____

4. Did graduates of Croaker College really win frog-jumping contests more often?

   _____

Critical Thinking

Discuss these questions with your classmates.

1. Have you ever heard of a special event taking place in China?
2. Describe an event that requires special clothing or costumes.
3. Is there any value in such an unusual event as the Jumping Frog Contest? Explain why.
4. If you had a chance to create an unusual contest, what would it be?
5. Do traditions and customs still have a significant influence on today's society? Why or why not?

Writing

Writing Skills

The Introduction

The *introduction* of an essay has two parts: *general statements* and a *thesis statement*. The first statement in an introduction should be a general statement about the topic. The second statement should be less general; the third statement should be even less general, and so on until the reader comes to the thesis statement. The number of general statements you write in an introduction depends on how long your essay is. However, you should write at least two or three general statements in an introduction.

- **General statements** introduce the topic of the essay and give background information on the topic.

- The **thesis statement** is often the last sentence of the introduction. It is the most important sentence in the introduction. It gives the specific topic and the controlling ideas for the whole essay. It may list the subtopics that will be discussed in the body paragraphs, or state the method of organization of the essay.

Exercise 1

Read the following introductory paragraphs for essays describing a series of events on a special day. The sentences in these introductions are not in the correct order. Rewrite each introduction, beginning with the most general statement and ending with the thesis statement.

1. (1) Sometimes weddings are planned more than a year in advance because there are many events and procedures that must not be forgotten. (2) The traditional American wedding is formal and has many steps, each of which has a symbolic meaning. (3) Most people love their wedding day and remember it for the rest of their lives. (4) A great deal of preparation and expense go into planning a wedding.

2. (1) April Fools' Day is celebrated on the first day of April in most countries. (2) If, like me, you don't know what day it is, you may be in for a surprise. (3) It is a day when people have a lot of fun. (4) People often play tricks on each other. (5) Last April Fools' Day is a day I will never forget because three very surprising things happened to me.

3. (1) The reason for the festivities is explained in stories handed down through generations. (2) Ga Homowo is a festival of Thanksgiving celebrated by the Ga people of Ghana. (3) They had the first festival after the harvest, and now they celebrate it annually. (4) Unlike most annual festivals, Ga Homowo is made up of a series of events and celebrated within family groups. (5) These stories trace the origin of Ga Homowo to the first immigrants of the Ga tribe who landed on the shores of Ghana.

_____

_____

_____

_____

Exercise 2

Read the following essay written by a student. Then answer the questions at the end of the essay.

The Dragon Boat Festival

The Dragon Boat Festival is a significant festival in Chinese traditional celebrations. The Dragon Boat Festival is celebrated on the fifth day of lunar May. This holiday is to commemorate the death of Qu Yuan, a well-loved poet of the fourth century B.C. Qu Yuan drowned himself to protest his king's despotic rule. The villagers respected him so much that they rowed their boats down the river and dropped *tzung-tzu*, "rice dumplings", into the river to feed Qu Yuan's spirit. To celebrate the Dragon Boat Festival, families do several things, such as making tzung-tzu, hanging the moxa herb, and watching the dragon boat race.

Before the Dragon Boat Festival, every family prepares tzung-tzu. This is a kind of rice dumpling filled with various things, such as bean curd, meat, mushrooms, and shrimp, and it is then wrapped in bamboo leaves and steamed. The mother and the children all work together in preparing the tzung-tzu.

Then each family also has to buy moxa herb and hang it in a special location. The reason for this is that the moxa herb can get rid of the bad luck. Some people even use these herbs to wash sick babies, for they believe that this special festival can bring some "transformation" in people's lives. Usually the father and the boys find a location to hang the moxa herb.

After preparing the tzung-tzu, each family goes to the river to watch the dragon boat race, which takes place during this festival. The dragon boat race symbolizes the story of Qu Yuan. It is a rowing boat team competition with about 30 people on each team. All the spectators cheer and shout enthusiastically. After the exciting race, both the competitors and the spectators usually eat many tzung-tzu.

Dragon boats race on the river in Foshan City, China.

The Dragon Boat Festival symbolizes the unique meanings of Chinese history; furthermore, the process of making the rice dumplings, the hanging of the moxa herb, and the boat race are a way of drawing all members of the family together again. Perhaps one day we will have a very different celebration, but so far I still like this holiday being celebrated in a traditional way.

1. What is the thesis statement for the whole essay? Where is it located? Circle it.
2. What are the topic sentences in each of the body paragraphs? Underline them.
3. Do each of the body paragraphs have supporting sentences?

The Conclusion

The final paragraph of your essay is the *conclusion*. It tells the reader you have completed your essay.

- You can begin your conclusion with a transition signal such as:

    In conclusion, ...   *In summary, ...*   *To summarize, ...*

- In the conclusion, you either summarize the main points in the body of your essay or rewrite the thesis statement using different words. Then you can add a final comment or thought on the subject.

Exercise 3

Write conclusions for essays with the following introductions. The first one is done for you.

1.

Introduction

On October 31, Americans celebrate Halloween. Halloween means "holy evening". This is the evening before the Christian holy day of All Saints' Day. However, Halloween is older than Christianity. Before Christianity, people in Britain believed that the ghosts of the dead came back on this day, and so they had rituals to scare the ghosts. Immigrants came from Europe to America and brought with them the custom of Halloween, as well as many symbols and activities associated with this day.

Conclusion

In conclusion, Halloween as it is celebrated in the United States today still has many symbols and rituals brought over by the European immigrants. Although it is an old of fun. People will continue to celebrate Halloween for a long time to come.

2.

Introduction

Like other countries, Japan has its own strict rules for table manners. These rules date back to the sixteenth century, when the Ogasawara system of manners was developed. With the creation of this system, table manners reached an art form. These rules involve how the food is served, how the chopsticks are handled, and the order in which the foods are eaten.

Conclusion

_____
_____
_____

3.

Introduction

Birthday celebrations have been around for more than 5,000 years. In every part of the world, birthdays are celebrated in a slightly different way. The traditional American birthday celebration was brought over by the Europeans. The elements, such as a birthday song, a cake, candles, and gifts, are symbolic. In the United States, many birthday celebrations involve these elements.

Conclusion

_____
_____
_____

Exercise 4

Reread the student essay "The Dragon Boat Festival" on Pages 39–40. Then work with a partner and discuss whether or not the student has written an effective conclusion. Has the student summarized the main points, rewritten the thesis statement, or added a final comment?

Writing Practice

Write Paragraphs

Choose one of the following topics to write an introduction and a conclusion of an essay.

1. A holiday custom
2. An unusual event
3. My favorite celebration

Pre-Write

A Work with a partner and brainstorm examples for your topic.

B Make a list of your examples, and work on a thesis statement for your introduction paragraph.

Outline

Fill in the outline below. Write your thesis statement for an essay, and pick three examples from Exercise B in Pre-Write for the introduction and conclusion paragraphs. Use these examples as your general statements.

Paragraph Outline

Introduction Paragraph

General statement 1: _____

General statement 2: _____

General statement 3: _____

Thesis statement: _____

_____

Conclusion Paragraph

Restate thesis or summarize main points: _____

_____

Final comment: _____

Write and Revise Your Paragraphs

Translation

A Translate the following passage into English.

每年农历八月十五是我国的传统节日——中秋节。这是一年秋季的中期,所以被称为中秋。中秋节的一项重要活动是赏月。夜晚,人们赏明月、吃月饼,共庆中秋佳节。中秋节也是家庭团圆的节日,远在他乡的游子,会借此寄托自己对故乡和亲人的思念之情。形式多样的中秋习俗,都寄托着人们对美好生活的热爱和向往。

B Translate the following passage into Chinese.

Paper cutting is one of China's most popular traditional folk arts. Chinese paper cutting has a history of more than 1,500 years. It was widespread particularly during the Ming and Qing Dynasties. People often use it to make their homes more beautiful. During the Spring Festival and wedding celebrations, in particular, paper cuttings are used to decorate doors, windows and rooms in order to increase the festive atmosphere. The color most frequently used in paper cutting is red, which symbolizes health and prosperity. Chinese paper cutting is very popular around the world and is often given as a present to foreign friends.

Weaving It Together

Unit Project

In this part, you are required to do some research among your classmates, friends or relatives. Collect information about a traditional Chinese festival. Then give a presentation to your classmates. The following questions can be used as references.

1. What is the origin of the festival?
2. Do people need to wear any festive clothes?
3. What kind of festive food should be prepared?
4. Is the holiday celebrated in the same way throughout China?
5. What is the symbol of the festival?

Searching the Internet

A Search the Internet for information about the festivals: Obon, Inti Raymi, and Fasching. Find answers to these questions:

1. Where is the festival celebrated?
2. When is it celebrated?
3. What do people do during the festival?

B Search the Internet for information about unusual customs or traditions around the world. Share the information with your classmates.

What Do You Think Now?

Refer to Page 25 at the beginning of this unit. Do you know the answers now? Complete the sentence, or circle the best answer.

1. Hawaii (is/isn't) an independent country with its own language and culture.
2. Different cultures in the United States (celebrate/don't celebrate) Thanksgiving in different ways.
3. _____ people attended a frog-jumping contest in California.
4. Competitors (can/can't) rent or bring their own frogs to the contest.

Broadening Your Horizon

Thanksgiving Day in the United States

Thanksgiving Day in the United States is a holiday on the fourth Thursday of November. It precedes Black Friday. Thanksgiving Day is traditionally a day for families and friends to get together for a special meal. The meal often includes a turkey, stuffing, potatoes, cranberry sauce, gravy, pumpkin pie, and vegetables. Thanksgiving Day is a time for many people to give thanks for what they have.

B

Thanksgiving in Hawaii

Being able to celebrate Thanksgiving in Hawaii is something to be thankful for! If you are looking for an alternative to the traditional turkey dinner, it is not too late to reserve a spot at some of the best Thanksgiving activities in Hawaii. This is our list of fun ways to spend Thanksgiving in Hawaii.

C

The Celebrated Jumping Frog of Calaveras County

"The Celebrated Jumping Frog of Calaveras County" is an 1865 short story by Mark Twain. It was his first great success as a writer and brought him national attention. The story has also been published as "Jim Smiley and His Jumping Frog" (its original title) and "The Notorious Jumping Frog of Calaveras County". In it, the narrator retells a story he heard from a bartender, Simon Wheeler, at the Angels Hotel in Angels Camp, California, about the gambler Jim Smiley. The narrator describes him, "If he even seen a straddle bug start to go anywhere, he would bet you how long it would take him to get to wherever he going to, and if you took him up, he would foller that straddle bug to Mexico but what he would find out where he was bound for and how long he was on the road."

UNIT 3
Mind and Body

A man practices tai chi on Victoria Peak, overlooking Victoria Harbor, Hong Kong, China.

WHAT DO YOU THINK?

Answer these questions with your best guess. Circle *Yes* or *No*.

1. Did the ancient Greeks believe that a person's features, such as the shape of the head, could tell about a person's character?   Yes   No
2. Does a theory called phrenology use lines on the head to tell character?   Yes   No
3. Do elderly people who have pets live longer?   Yes   No
4. Can dogs smell cancer in humans?   Yes   No

Reading 1

Pre-Reading

Preparing for the Reading Topic

A Discuss these questions with your classmates.

1. Do people have differently shaped heads? What does a person's head shape tell you about the person?

2. What can you tell about the man in the photo on Page 50 by looking at his face and the bumps on his head?

3. Do some people's faces look like birds or animals? In what ways?

B Which parts of the head and face do you associate with each of the following characteristics? Match each part with a characteristic. Then after you have read "Personality Revealed", review your answers.

_____ 1. nose   a. curiosity

_____ 2. lips   b. self-confidence

_____ 3. eyes   c. decisiveness

_____ 4. shape of face d. creativity

_____ 5. eyebrows   e. pride

Key Vocabulary

As you read "Personality Revealed", pay attention to the following words and see if you can work out their meanings from the context.

reveals	prominent
traits	indicates
stern	bulge
courageous	ridiculed
arrogant	bitter

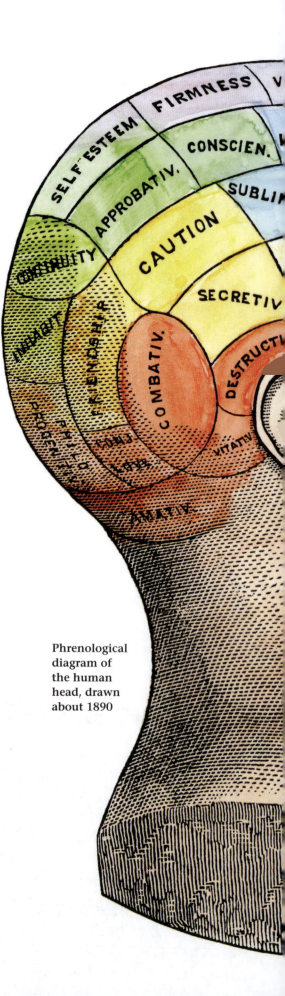

Phrenological diagram of the human head, drawn about 1890

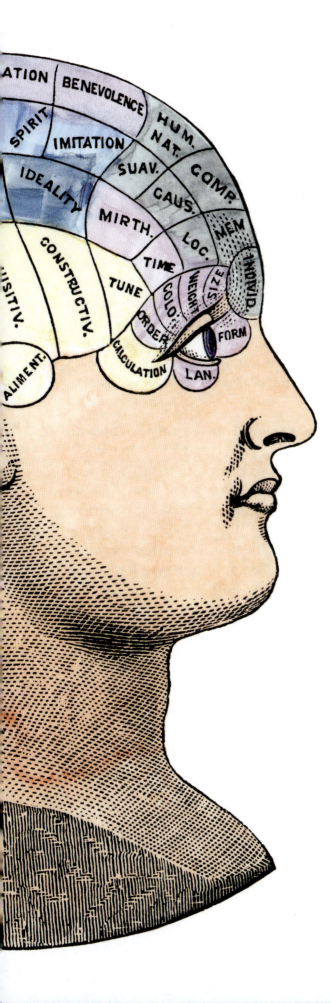

Personality REVEALED

1   Have you ever been afraid of or attracted to someone just because of the way the person looks? When you first meet someone, it is not unusual to react to his or her appearance. But these are first impressions, and most people assume that it takes time to find out what someone is really like. It is possible, however, that a person's appearance **reveals** more than we realize. According to some people, a person's face, head, and body can reveal a great deal about personality.

2   Since ancient times, people have practiced the art of physiognomy[1], or reading character from physical features. The ancient Greeks compared the human face to the faces of various animals and birds, such as the eagle and the horse. They believed people shared certain character **traits** with the animals they resembled. A person with an equine[2] or horse-like face was thought to be loyal, brave and **stern**. A person with an aquiline[3] or eagle-like nose was believed to be bold and **courageous**, as well as **arrogant** and self-centered.

3   Physiognomists study such features as the shape of the head, the length and thickness of the neck, the color and thickness of the hair, and the shape of the nose, mouth, eyes, and chin. They believe that round-faced people are self-confident. **Prominent** cheekbones show strength

---

1 physiognomy 面相学
2 equine 马的，像马的
3 aquiline 鹰的，像鹰的

of character, while a pointed nose reveals curiosity. Heavy, arched eyebrows belong to a decisive individual, while thin, arched eyebrows signal a restless and active personality. Almond-shaped eyes reveal an artistic nature. Round, soft eyes belong to dreamers. Down-turned lips reveal a proud character, while a long, pointed chin **indicates** someone who likes to give orders.

4   A related—though not as ancient—art is phrenology[4]. A couple of centuries ago, phrenologists started studying the bumps on the human head. They were able to identify 40 bumps of various shapes and sizes. They "read" these bumps to identify a person's talents and character. For example, a bump between the nose and forehead was said to be present in people who had natural elegance and a love of beauty. A bump behind the curve of the ear was the sign of a courageous and adventurous person.

5   Phrenologists were not so much interested in health as they were in character and personality. They believed, for example, that a **bulge** in the center of the forehead was typical of people who had a good memory and a desire for knowledge. A small bump at the top of the head indicated a person who had strong moral character, while a bump just below this one was a sign of generosity and a kind, good nature. Phrenologists believed that a bump just above the tip of the eyebrow was found in people who loved order and discipline, and a rise at the very back of the head was evident in people who were very attached to their families.

6   Phrenology was developed in the early eighteenth century by Franz Joseph Gall[5], a doctor in Vienna. His interest began at school when he noticed that boys with prominent eyes seemed to have the best memories. This led him to believe that a connection existed between appearance and ability. Dr. Gall's research interested many people, but he was **ridiculed** by other doctors. When he died in 1828, he was a poor and **bitter** man. After his death, however, phrenology achieved some popularity in the second half of the nineteenth century, and today there are still a few phrenologists even though there is no scientific evidence to support its practice.

---

4 phrenology 颅相学
5 Franz Joseph Gall 弗朗兹·约瑟夫·加尔

Vocabulary

Vocabulary in Context

A What are the meanings of the **bold** words? Circle the letter of the best answer.

1. A person's face **reveals** a great deal about personality.
   - a. shows
   - b. covers up
   - c. holds
   - d. identifies

2. The ancient Greeks believed that people shared certain character **traits** with animals.
   - a. features
   - b. movements
   - c. styles
   - d. connections

3. A person with a horse-like face might be proud and **stern**.
   - a. noble
   - b. serious
   - c. quiet
   - d. confident

4. A **courageous** person is not afraid in dangerous situations.
   - a. strong
   - b. intelligent
   - c. brave
   - d. cautious

5. A person with an eagle-like nose was believed to be **arrogant** and self-centered.
   - a. honest
   - b. proud
   - c. lonely
   - d. brave

6. **Prominent** cheekbones show strength of character.
   - a. healthy
   - b. hollow
   - c. noticeable
   - d. flat

7. A long, pointed chin **indicates** someone who likes to give orders.
   - a. covers up
   - b. points out
   - c. encourages
   - d. describes

8. A **bulge** in the center of the forehead is typical of people with a good memory.
   - a. bump
   - b. hole
   - c. point
   - d. mark

9. Dr. Gall was **ridiculed** by other doctors.
   - a. praised
   - b. questioned
   - c. ignored
   - d. laughed at

10. He died a poor and **bitter** man.
    - a. hopeful
    - b. unhappy
    - c. faithful
    - d. popular

B Answer these questions with complete sentences.

1. Would you ever **reveal** a friend's secret to another person?

2. How does a **stern** teacher look and act?

3. How would you describe an **arrogant** person?

4. What does a smile **indicate** in your culture?

5. How does it feel to be **ridiculed**?

C Now write your own sentences. Use the following words in the sentences: **traits**, **courageous**, **prominent**, **bulge**, and **bitter**.

_____

_____

_____

Vocabulary Building

Complete these sentences with the correct form of the **bold** words. You may use your dictionary.

1. courageous
   a. The shape of his nose showed that he was a man of _____.
   b. The man swam _____ to help the boy in the river.

2. indicate
   a. Down-turned lips _____ that a person is proud.
   b. A pointed chin is an _____ that the person likes to give orders.

3. reveal
   a. It is believed by some that a person's facial features _____ a lot about their character.
   b. People were shocked at the _____ of the famous couple's divorce.

Reading Comprehension

A Circle the letter of the best answer.

1. Which of the following best expresses the main idea of this passage?
   a. Learning about the relationship between human and animal.
   b. Learning about the theory of physiognomy.
   c. Learning about the history of physiognomy.
   d. Learning about some famous physiognomists.

2. What do physiognomists believe?
   a. They believe you can improve your personality by studying your face.
   b. They believe the head is the most important part of the body.
   c. Physical features reveal personality.
   d. People are like animals in many ways.

3. Which one is true about phrenologists?
   a. They "read" the bumps on people's heads to treat their health problems.
   b. They compared bumps on heads to see who was more attractive.
   c. They believed the eyes were the "mirror of the soul".
   d. They studied bumps on the head to determine character traits.

4. Which of the following is true about Dr. Gall's ideas?

   a. They were at first not accepted by other doctors.

   b. They were immediately considered the work of a genius.

   c. They are no longer discussed.

   d. They made him admired in his lifetime.

5. What's the author's attitude toward phrenology?

   a. Positive.

   b. Negative.

   c. Objective.

   d. Indifferent.

B Each of the following statements contains information given in the passage. Identify the paragraph from which the information is derived.

1. Physiognomy is an ancient practice.   Paragraph _____

2. Dr. Gall was not rewarded for his research in his lifetime.   Paragraph _____

3. A bump behind the curve of the ear shows that these people are courageous and adventurous.   Paragraph _____

4. It's usual to react to one's looking when you meet someone for the first time.   Paragraph _____

5. The ancient Greeks compared the human face to the faces of various animals.   Paragraph _____

6. Phrenologists could identify 40 bumps of various shapes and sizes.   Paragraph _____

7. A person with a bulge in the center of the forehead usually has a good memory and a desire for knowledge. Paragraph _____

8. Round-faced people are regarded self-confident by physiognomists.   Paragraph _____

Critical Thinking

Discuss these questions with your classmates.

1. What characteristics of the face and body show good health? What characteristics show bad health?

2. Do you think that astrology is more precise than physiognomy or phrenology? Explain why.

3. Look at your partner. What do the characteristics of your partner's face reveal about his or her personality?

4. In what ways does today's society emphasize physical appearance? Do you think there is too much emphasis on physical appearance today? Why or why not?

5. What does it mean to have "inner beauty"? Can you tell if a person has inner beauty from their outward appearance? How do you know if a person has inner beauty?

Reading 2

Pre-Reading

Preparing for the Reading Topic

A Discuss these questions with your classmates.

1. Do you have a pet? Why or why not?
2. If you have a pet, what kind is it? Does your pet make you feel good? Explain how.
3. If you don't have a pet but would like one, what kind would you like?
4. Do you think pets are good for people? Why or why not?

B Imagine you are an elderly person living alone. Which of the following would you choose to make you happy? Check two. Then explain why.

_____ a computer   _____ visitors

_____ a pet   _____ TV

Key Vocabulary

As you read "Pets to the Rescue", pay attention to the following words and phrases and see if you can work out their meanings from the context.

treated	emotionally disturbed
significantly	do wonders
overall	nursing homes
heart attack	pet
cope with	detect

Pets to the Rescue

A therapy dog visits a young girl in the hospital.

1   When you walk into a hospital room, you expect to see a nurse or a doctor. But in some hospitals you might also see a dog or a cat, or even a rabbit or a turtle. These pets aren't there to be **treated**, however. They're part of the medical team! The animals don't have medical degrees, of course. They help patients get better simply by being there.

2   After 30 years of study, researchers are convinced that animals provide many health benefits. These range from lowering blood pressure to faster healing after surgery. One study shows that even 10 minutes with an animal can **significantly** lower blood

pressure. There are many examples of how pets improve people's health. For instance, studies show that pet owners have lower cholesterol[1] levels than non-owners do. Pet owners are also in better physical health **overall** and have fewer doctor visits. Also, people who have suffered a **heart attack** live longer if they have a pet. And pet owners have better mental health because pets make them happier, more relaxed, and less stressed.

3   Did you have a pet as a child? Do your grandparents own a pet? The health benefits of pets are quite strong for both children and the elderly. For example, a pet can help children **cope with** family problems, such as illness or the death of a relative. Studies also show that children who own pets are more likely to be involved in sports and hobbies. **Emotionally disturbed** and mentally ill children are also helped greatly by pets. Animals calm children and improve their behavior and even their mental abilities. Animals **do wonders** for the elderly too, such as helping them live longer, healthier lives. How do they do this? For one thing, pets make older people feel less lonely and depressed. And some pets, such as dogs, encourage elders to exercise by getting out for walks. Some aid groups take pets into **nursing homes** to cheer up the residents. Pets bring out smiles of happiness from elders and help improve their quality of life.

4   Some groups also bring pets into hospitals. Most often, the animals are dogs, but they can also be cats, rabbits, birds, and others. They are called therapy animals. These animals are trained to give comfort and affection to patients. Good therapy animals are friendly, gentle, and patient. They allow people to **pet** and talk to them. They bring laughter and enjoyment to sick people and help them feel better.

5   There are quite a few animal healing programs today. One interesting example is the Dolphin Program. Researchers at universities and dolphin centers worldwide study the healing effects of swimming with dolphins. Some researchers believe that the sounds dolphins make underwater can heal people. Others say dolphins heal because they make people feel peaceful and happy. Dolphin programs for children with special needs have been very successful. Even patients with serious illnesses improve by swimming with dolphins.

6   Another interesting example of animals helping sick people is a program that uses dogs to **detect** cancer. Researchers have found that dogs can smell cancer in patients' breath because it contains certain chemicals. A dog's sense of smell is 10,000 to 100,000 times better than that of human's. In studies, trained dogs have identified cancer in early stages between 88 and 97 percent of the time. Since detecting cancer early is important to a patient's survival, these trained dogs could save many lives.

7   Researchers know that animals make people feel better and extend their lives. But they can't fully explain why. They suspect it's because people can count on pets to be there, always loving and never judging. This gives people a good feeling and relaxes them. Patients feel calm and happy around pets. This mental and emotional state helps them feel better physically. Whatever the reasons, there is no doubt that animals are good medicine for people of all ages. Pets have a valuable place in homes, hospitals, and all places of care.

---

1 cholesterol 胆固醇

Vocabulary

A Complete these sentences with the words and phrases in the box.

| cope with | do wonders | heart attack | overall | significantly |
| detect | emotionally disturbed | nursing homes | pet | treated |

1. When a person gets medical help in a hospital, he or she is _____.
2. When something changes to an important degree, it changes _____.
3. _____ is considering everything.
4. A medical condition in which a person's heart suddenly stops beating is a(n) _____.
5. To deal with something successfully is to _____ it.
6. People who are _____ cannot behave normally because they have problems of the mind.
7. When things _____, they have a very good effect.
8. _____ are places for people who are too old or too ill to take care of themselves.
9. To move your hand over an animal's fur is to _____ the animal.
10. When you notice something that is not easy to see or hear, you _____ it.

B Answer these questions with complete sentences.

1. Do people live **significantly** longer today than 100 years ago?

2. What difficult situations have you had to **cope with** in your life?

3. What exercises **do wonders** for your health?

4. Do many people in your country go into **nursing homes** when they get old?

5. Which animals do you like to **pet** and which do you not like to **pet**?

C Now write your own sentences. Use the following words and phrases in the sentences: *treat*, *overall*, *emotionally disturbed*, and *detect*.

Unit 3 Mind and Body

Reading Comprehension

A Circle the letter of the best answer.

1. Which of the following best expresses the main idea of this passage?
   a. How pets help both children and the elderly.
   b. People who own pets live longer.
   c. The benefits of laughter pets bring to people.
   d. The therapeutic and healing effects of pets.

2. What could we infer from the second paragraph?
   a. Pets help to lower people's blood pressure.
   b. Pet owners see doctors less often than non-owners.
   c. Pets help people to be happier and more relaxed.
   d. Owning pets has several healthful benefits.

3. What could be inferred from the fifth paragraph?
   a. There are many animal healing programs today.
   b. The Dolphin Program studies how swimming with dolphins heals people.
   c. Researchers believe that people are healed by the sounds the dolphins make.
   d. The Dolphin Program has proven to be helpful to children with special needs.

4. What does the author intend to show by stating that pet owners have fewer doctor visits?
   a. Pet owners could send their animals to doctors.
   b. Pets could improve people's health.
   c. Pets could replace doctors.
   d. Pets could cure all kinds of illness.

5. Which animals are used for therapy in hospitals most often?
   a. Cats.
   b. Birds.
   c. Dogs.
   d. Rabbits.

B Complete the sentences below with words from the passage. Use NO MORE THAN THREE WORDS for each answer.

1. Pets are good _____ for people of all ages.

2. Patients could get _____ from the trained animals.

3. A dog's _____ is 10,000 to 100,000 times better than that of humans.

4. Researches show that pet owners have _____ cholesterol levels than those who don't have pets.

5. Different researchers have various explanations for the _____ of swimming with dolphins.

6. Lots of elderly people are encouraged to _____ by walking outside.

Critical Thinking

Discuss these questions with your classmates.

1. What animals other than a cat or dog do people have as pets? Do these animals help the owners feel better? Explain why.

2. What is an interesting or remarkable story that you have read, heard, or experienced about how an animal helped a human?

3. Dolphins are one of the most researched animals on the earth. Do you think why dolphins attract so much attention? How have they been used other than in healing programs?

4. What are the advantages and disadvantages of owning a pet?

5. Do you think that pets can actually heal people? Why or why not?

Writing

Writing Skills

The Example Essay

In an *example essay*, each body paragraph gives examples to support the thesis statement in the introduction. Examples are introduced with transition words.

- To give examples, use the following transitions at the beginning of your body paragraphs:

  Body paragraph 1: **One example** of [noun phrase] is…
  Take… **for example,**…
  An example of [noun phrase] is…

  Body paragraph 2: **Another example** of [noun phrase] is…
  An additional example is…
  A second example of [noun phrase] is…

  Body paragraph 3: **A final example** of [noun phrase] is…
  Finally,…

- If your next example is the most important, use the following transitions:

  The **most important example** of [noun phrase] is…
  The **most significant / interesting example** of [noun phrase] is…

- In your body paragraphs, you may use other specific examples to support the topic sentence of a body paragraph. The following transitions introduce examples:

  For example,…
  For instance,…

- **For example** and **for instance** have the same meaning. When your sentence begins with **for example** or **for instance**, put a comma after these words. Remember that when **for example** or **for instance** comes at the beginning of a sentence, it must be followed by a complete sentence.

  EXAMPLES: **For example,** it helps me to study when the lesson is difficult.
  For instance, I like everything to be neat and tidy.

- Sometimes **e.g.** is used to show examples; it is an abbreviation of the Latin *exempli gratia*. **For example** and **e.g.** have the same meaning. Note the punctuation with **e.g.**

  EXAMPLES: I am very patient with people, too, **e.g.,** with children and senior citizens.
  I am very patient with people, too, **for example,** with children and senior citizens.

- When **for example**, **for instance**, or **e.g.** is used in the middle of a sentence, use commas before and after these words.

- For further examples, you may use **also** or **another**.

Exercise 1

Complete the following sentences by adding the correct transitions. There may be more than one correct answer.

The left and right sides of the face are quite different. Each side shows different aspects of our personality. The left side of the face reveals the instinctive and hereditary aspects of our personality. When we are under stress, 1._____, with feelings like fear, anger, or even intense happiness, force is put on the muscles of the left side of the face. When we examine the left side of the face, our well-being and troubles show up more. 2._____, wrinkles on this side show the strong emotions we have experienced in our lives. The right side of the face reflects our intelligence and self-control. This side of the face is usually more relaxed and smoother. That is why, 3._____, movie stars prefer to have this side of their face photographed.

Exercise 2

Read the following example essay written by a student. Then answer the questions at the end of the essay.

A Virgo

Every person has both good and bad character traits. Most people do not like to be criticized by others. However, it is good to be honest with yourself. We must admit that we all have both good and bad traits, and we must like ourselves as we are. If people do not love even a part of themselves, then they are practically dead. Since I am going to write about myself, I will write about the good and bad traits of my character. I was born under the astrological sign Virgo, and I believe I have some of the characteristics of people born under this sign.

One example of a good trait of a Virgo that I have is patience. Sometimes I think I am almost too patient, but I have also found that patience helps me with a lot of things. For example, it helps me to study when the lesson is difficult or boring. Also, if I don't succeed in something, I am willing to try several more times. My patience also helps me to relax and stay calm. I am very patient with people, too, e.g., with children, senior citizens, and even people who are sick and need a lot of help. I can deal with people who are nervous, angry, and upset, and help them to calm down. Sometimes people take advantage of my patience, however, and I don't like that at all.

Another example of a typical Virgo trait that I have is ambition. I am very ambitious and can't sit in one place for more than 10 minutes. If I make up my mind to do something, then I will do anything to meet my goal. It doesn't matter how long it takes and how much energy and time will be needed to accomplish it. This is what helped me to graduate from high school in three years. I like to do housework, cook, and take care of babies. I also like to work outside my home. I like to be busy all day and have lots of things to do. This makes me happy and satisfied. I hate sitting at home all day doing nothing.

> Finally, like anyone, Virgos have some bad traits, too. Ambition can sometimes make them take on more work than they can handle, leading them to strain themselves to a breaking point. Sometimes I take on too much work and then reach a point at which I can do no more. Then I have to rest for a while and regain my strength. Virgos can also be fussy and irritable. I suppose I can be that way, too, sometimes. For instance, I like everything to be neat and tidy. If someone comes along and messes things up, I will scold them.
>
> In conclusion, I am very happy that I am a Virgo. My patience and ambition gave me the confidence I needed to choose to be a psychologist. Because I work hard and can deal with people who have problems, I think I will someday be very successful in this profession. Some people envy me for the traits I have, and that gives me an idea that I am not so bad after all.

1. Where is the thesis statement? Circle it.
2. What is the topic sentence in each of the body paragraphs? Underline it.
3. What transitions are used at the beginning and in the middle of the paragraphs to introduce examples? Double underline them.

Using *such as*

One way to introduce an example is by the use of **such as**. We use **such as** + example when we want to be brief.

> EXAMPLES: Owning a pet can help children cope with family problems, **such as** illness or the death of a relative.
>
> Some pets, **such as** dogs, encourage elders to exercise by getting out for walks.
>
> Studies **such as** these make us appreciate pets.

- No commas are needed when the **such as** phrase gives essential information. Use commas when the **such as** phrase can be taken out without changing the meaning of the sentence.

Exercise 3

Combine the two sentences into one using **such as**. Use correct punctuation. The first one is done for you.

1. Studies show that pets provide a range of health benefits. For instance, pets help in lowering blood pressure and faster healing after surgery.

   Studies show that pets provide a range of health benefits, such as lowering blood pressure and faster healing after surgery.

2. Children get many benefits from pet ownership. For example, owning a pet helps them cope with family illness and death.

   _____

   _____

3. Healing programs use many different animals. For instance, these programs use dogs, cats, rabbits, and birds to help the sick feel better.

4. Today there are quite a few animal healing programs. For example, there is the Dolphin Program and a program that uses dogs to detect cancer.

5. Studies show that pets do wonders for the elderly. For example, pets help the elderly feel less lonely and encourage them to exercise.

6. Owning pets improves people's health in several ways. For instance, pet owners have lower cholesterol levels and lower blood pressure, which can help extend their lives.

Exercise 4

Punctuate these sentences containing examples, where necessary.

1. Pet-owning children for instance tend to be calmer.
2. Birds for example are easy for the elderly to love and care for.
3. Not all animal healing programs use dogs for example the Dolphin Program doesn't.
4. Some pets are brought into medical facilities such as nursing homes.
5. For instance some nursing homes let their residents have cats.
6. A remedy such as pet ownership is very helpful.

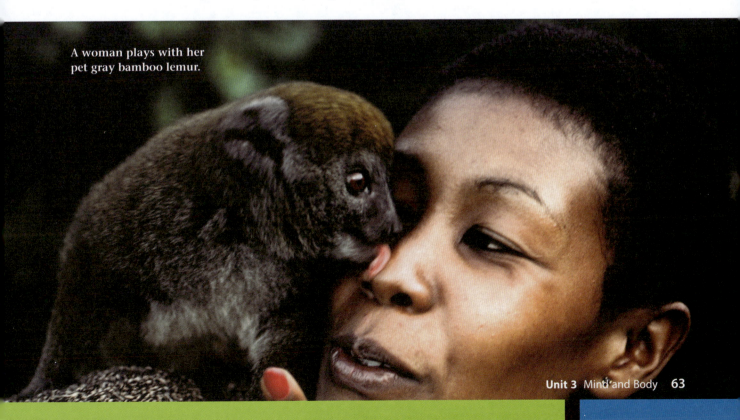

A woman plays with her pet gray bamboo lemur.

Writing Practice

Write an Essay

Choose one of the following topics to write an example essay.

1. The different ways animals help people
2. The benefits of practicing yoga
3. The benefits of exercise on the body and mind
4. How a healthy diet and exercise are good for the body

Pre-Write

A Work with a partner and brainstorm examples for your topic.

B Make a list of your examples, and work on a thesis statement for your essay.

Outline

Fill in the outline below. Write your thesis statement for your essay, and pick the two best examples from Exercise B in Pre-Write for the supporting details in your body paragraphs. Finally, write your conclusion.

Essay Outline

Introduction

Thesis statement: _____

_____

Body Paragraph 1

Topic sentence: _____

_____

Supporting detail 1: _____

Supporting detail 2: _____

Body Paragraph 2

Topic sentence: _____

_____

Supporting detail 1: _____

Supporting detail 2: _____

Conclusion

Restatement of thesis or summary of main points: _____

_____

Final comment: _____

Write and Revise Your Essay

Translation

A Translate the following passage into English.

有些大学要求学生每天早上六点半到七点跑800米，一个学期至少50次。对于一些习惯学习到很晚的学生来说，这种规定让他们很难平衡作息规律。如果他们要保持原来晚上学习的习惯，第二天早上肯定很难起床去跑步。再者，休息不足也会影响第二天的学习。我们可以想象他们深夜学习的辛苦，他们自己也会发现白天的学习效率会有所下降。

B Translate the following passage into Chinese.

Body language is used by people for sending messages to each other. It is very useful because it can help you make yourself easily understood. When you are talking with others, you are using not only words, but also expressions and gestures. For example, raising your hand is to say "Good-bye". A smile and handshake is to welcome people, and clapping hands means congratulations. Nodding the head means agreement, and shaking the head means disagreement. These gestures are accepted both by the Chinese and foreigners as having the same meanings. When you use a foreign language, it is very important to know the meanings of gestures in the foreign country. Following the customs will help you communicate with the local people and make your stay there much more pleasant and comfortable.

Weaving It Together

Unit Project

In this part, you are required to do some research among your classmates, friends or relatives. Collect information about appearance and character. Then give a presentation to your classmates. The following questions can be used as references.

1. Can you describe your friend's appearance?
2. Does the appearance of your friend reflect his or her character?
3. Have you ever judged a stranger by his or her appearance?
4. Is your first impression about a person always right?
5. How can you predict a person's character from his appearance?

Searching the Internet

A Search the Internet for information about phrenology. Find answers to these questions:

1. What is the history of phrenology?
2. Are there countries in which phrenology is still popular?
3. What do most scientists think of phrenology today?

B Search the Internet for three examples of programs that use pets as therapy to help people. Share the information with your classmates.

What Do You Think Now?

Refer to Page 47 at the beginning of this unit. Do you know the answers now? Complete the sentence, or circle the best answer.

1. The ancient Greeks (believed/did not believe) that a person's features, such as the shape of the head, could tell about a person's character.
2. A theory called phrenology uses _____ on the head to tell character.
3. Elderly people who have pets (live/don't live) longer.
4. Dogs (can/can't) smell cancer in humans.

Broadening Your Horizon

A

Physiognomy

Physiognomy (from the Greek, physis meaning "nature", and gnomon meaning "judge" or "interpreter") is the assessment of a person's character or personality from his or her outer appearance, especially the face. The term can also refer to the general appearance of a person, object, or terrain, without reference to its implied characteristics, as in the physiognomy of an individual plant (see plant life-form) or of a plant community (see vegetation).

B

Phrenology

Phrenology (from the Greek, phren meaning "mind", and logos meaning "knowledge") is a pseudo medicine, which primarily focuses on measurements of the human skull, based on the concept that the brain is the organ of the mind, and that certain brain areas have localized specific functions or modules.

C

Can Any Animal Be a Therapy Animal?

Dogs once cornered the market on being therapy pets, but now bunnies, pigs–even llamas–are making their way into the laps and hearts of people who have a range of conditions. But experts say some animals are more therapeutic than others.

"While we know that a wide variety of animals can be wonderful companions or pets, not every animal is suited to therapy work," said Glen Miller, a spokesman for Pet Partners, a national nonprofit organization that trains and registers therapy animals.

Therapy pets can include "dogs, cats, rabbits, birds, guinea pigs, rats, miniature pigs, llamas, alpacas, horses, donkeys and mini-horses", as long as they're at least a year old and have lived with their owner for six months, according to Pet Partners.

UNIT 4: People Making a Difference

Even after being shot by the Taliban in Pakistan in 2012, Malala Yousafzai (born in 1997) continues to speak out about the importance of education for young girls.

WHAT DO YOU THINK?

Answer these questions with your best guess. Circle *Yes* or *No*.

1. Is Africa losing its wild places and animals?   Yes   No
2. Is it easy to photograph wild animals?   Yes   No
3. Can girls go to school everywhere in the world?   Yes   No
4. Is it possible for one woman to build a school?   Yes   No

Reading 1

Pre-Reading

Preparing for the Reading Topic

A Discuss these questions with your classmates.

1. What are some countries that are famous for their wild animals?

2. What dangers do wild animals face from humans?

3. Who is a famous person of the past or present working to save wild animals? What special animal did that person want to protect?

Dereck and Beverly Joubert in Selinda Reserve, Botswana

B Check (✓) the following items that you associate with a wildlife area in Africa. Then after you have read "Saving Africa's Largest Animals", review your answers.

_____ brick houses   _____ insects

_____ crocodiles   _____ lions

_____ elephants   _____ roads

_____ heat   _____ snow

Key Vocabulary

As you read "Saving Africa's Largest Animals", pay attention to the following words and see if you can work out their meanings from the context.

daring   scratch

dedicated   patience

mission   disturb

tents   passionate

conservation   inspires

Saving Africa's Largest Animals

1   The temperature is 120 degrees Fahrenheit (48.8℃). Dereck and Beverly Joubert are standing next to their vehicle in Africa. A lion is coming toward them, looking for shade under a tree. Anyone else would run for their lives, but not the Jouberts. As the lion lies down near them, Dereck leans close to take a photo while Beverly holds him by his belt for safety. It's just another day in the life of this **daring** and **dedicated** couple.

2   Dereck and Beverly Joubert are South African filmmakers who have won many awards. Beverly is also a famous photographer. For over 30 years, they have dedicated their lives to filmmaking, research, and exploration in Africa. Their **mission** is to save and understand Africa's largest animals and other wildlife.

3   The Jouberts live in the African bush, far from any village. Often they don't see people for long periods of time. They sleep in **tents** and wake every morning at 4 a.m. to follow the animals. Sometimes they work all night to film animals in the dark. For thousands of hours, they filmed the lions for their greatest film, *The Last Lions*, and lived in some very difficult conditions. All their hard work to make the film was dedicated to the **conservation** of the lion population. So far, the Jouberts have made 25 films for *National Geographic*[1], published 11 books, and written many scientific papers and articles.

4   As well as being dedicated, the Jouberts are daring. While they were filming *The Last Lions*, they drove through water every morning to get to where they were going to film. More than once, their vehicle sank and they had to swim through waters with hungry crocodiles, waters that even lions were afraid to go into. When the Jouberts weren't swimming with crocodiles, they were living among rhinos, buffalo, leopards and lions. They slept in tents or in their vehicle and didn't even have doors to protect them. Lions have run toward them many times. The lions have come out of nowhere, roaring and kicking up dust right in the Jouberts' faces. Unbelievably, the Jourberts have never had even a **scratch** from a lion.

5   **Patience** is another quality the Jouberts have a lot of. Because they don't want to **disturb** the animals in any way, it takes them years to make a film. To make *The Last Lions*, they followed a lioness for seven years to tell the story of her fight to survive alone with her three baby cubs. When the Jouberts are making a film, they go out every day, sometimes for 16 hours or more. They sit quietly, hiding in the bush with the heat and insects. Some days, they don't even get one picture. But after many days and months, their patience is rewarded. The animals don't notice them anymore. They become part of the natural environment. Even after a successful day of filming, the Jouberts must return to their tent and sit for many more hours editing their film and writing down their notes and observations.

6   The Jouberts are not only a patient couple, but they are a **passionate** one as well. Their desire to save Africa's wild animals is what **inspires** them to make their films, have photography exhibitions, and write books and articles. They put a lot of hard work into explaining their mission and into showing the world the importance of conservation. They speak passionately about the number of animals we have already lost. They tell people that we must do something now, before it is too late, before the rhinos, elephants, and lions are gone.

7   Determined to save Africa's animals and wild places, the Jouberts have started the Big Cats Initiative[2] with *National Geographic* for the protection of big cats, such as leopards and lions. They have also created a new company called Great Plains Conservation that brings people together to protect large areas of land in the wild places of Africa where the animals live. Already they have saved 1.8 million acres. Protecting the animals and where they live is a life-long mission for the Jouberts, and it needs dedication, daring, patience, and a great deal of passion.

---

1 *National Geographic* 国家地理（杂志名）
2 Big Cats Initiative 拯救猫科动物行动计划

Vocabulary

Vocabulary in Context

A What are the meanings of the **bold** words? Circle the letter of the best answer.

1. Dereck and Beverly Joubert are a **daring** couple who live in the bush in Africa.
   - a. kind
   - b. emotional
   - c. physically strong
   - d. very brave

2. The Jouberts' **mission** is to save Africa's wild animals.
   - a. a way of talking about things
   - b. a show of interest in a certain subject
   - c. a habit or way of doing things
   - d. a special duty or purpose a person has

3. Dereck and Beverly Joubert are **dedicated** to their mission in Africa.
   - a. working hard for an idea or purpose
   - b. showing love for something or someone
   - c. making ones ideas known to others
   - d. strong about one's beliefs

4. They sleep in **tents** in the bush.
   - a. houses made of stones
   - b. dwellings made high in the trees
   - c. shelters made of cloth held up by poles
   - d. protected areas surrounded by fences

5. They work for the **conservation** of lions in Africa.
   - a. control of the behavior of
   - b. studying and understanding the lives of
   - c. keeping safe from loss or injury
   - d. preventing the movement of

6. The Jouberts have never had a **scratch** from a lion.
   - a. a bite from the teeth of an animal
   - b. a cut or mark made with something sharp
   - c. an itch caused by contact with something
   - d. a great injury caused by an attack

7. The Jouberts show a lot of **patience** when they film animals in the wild.
   - a. the strength to suffer through harsh and dangerous conditions
   - b. the ability to stay calm during long waits or unpleasant situations
   - c. the talent to do the right thing in any situation
   - d. the intelligence to make the best decisions

8. They try not to **disturb** the wild animals.
   - a. upset the natural state of
   - b. do physical harm to
   - c. give too much attention to
   - d. have too much control over

9. The Jouberts are **passionate** about their work to save the lions.
   - a. have a high opinion of
   - b. have plans and dreams about
   - c. have strong feelings about
   - d. have a great ability to do

10. Their desire to protect wild animals **inspires** them to make films.
    - a. makes them sad about
    - b. gives them the skills for
    - c. stops them from doing
    - d. moves them to act

B Answer these questions with complete sentences.

1. When do people live in **tents**?
   _____
   _____

2. What common situations require **patience**?
   _____
   _____

3. What sport requires someone to be **daring**?
   _____
   _____

4. Which person **inspires** you in your life?
   _____
   _____

5. What can you get a **scratch** from?
   _____
   _____

C Now write your own sentences. Use the following words in the sentences: **dedicated**, **mission**, **conservation**, **disturb**, and **passionate**.
_____
_____
_____
_____
_____

Vocabulary Building

Complete these sentences with the correct form of the **bold** words. You may use your dictionary.

1. **patience**
   a. The young mother showed a lot of _____ with her child.
   b. The audience was _____ when the band was late coming to the stage.

2. **inspire**
   a. The speaker gave an _____ talk on how to help others in need.
   b. My brother was _____ by his teacher to study astronomy.

3. **disturb**
   a. My mother doesn't like to be _____ when she is doing her yoga exercises.
   b. There was a _____ in the class when a bird flew in through the open window.

Reading Comprehension

A Circle the letter of the best answer.

1. What did Dereck and Beverly Joubert dedicate their lives to?
    a. Exploring unknown parts of Africa.
    b. Saving Africa's lions and other wildlife.
    c. Making award-winning films about Africa.
    d. Adventuring in the wild.

2. Where did the Jouberts sleep in the bush?
    a. Houses made of stones.
    b. Dwellings made high in the trees.
    c. Shelters made of cloth held up by poles.
    d. Protected areas surrounded by fences.

3. While the Jouberts were filming *The Last Lions*, what happened?
    a. They were never in any great danger.
    b. They were able to complete the film in record time.
    c. They faced many hardships over a long period.
    d. They had to stop their observation and study of other wildlife.

4. What has never happened when the Jouberts faced lions?
    a. A bite from a lion.
    b. A cut or mark caused by a lion.
    c. An itch caused by contact with a lion.
    d. A serious injury caused by a lion attack.

5. What did the Jouberts do to save Africa's animals and wild places?
    a. They brought people together to protect large wild areas.
    b. They put many wild animals on exhibition around the world.
    c. They created companies to take animals out of the wild.
    d. They stopped making films and writing books.

B Each statement below contains information given in the passage. Identify the paragraph from which the information is derived.

1. The Jouberts formed a new company to protect large areas of land in the wild places.   Paragraph _____

2. The Jouberts try to become part of the natural environment.   Paragraph _____

3. The Jouberts film animals during daylight and in the dark.   Paragraph _____

4. More than once, the Jouberts had to swim through waters with hungry crocodiles.   Paragraph _____

5. The Jouberts tell people that they must take actions before the wild animals disappear. Paragraph _____

6. The Jouberts' mission is to save and learn Africa's largest animals and other wildlife. Paragraph _____

Critical Thinking

Discuss these questions with your classmates.

1. Would you like to live and work in the wild like the Jouberts? Why or why not?
2. What are some reasons why the world is losing wild animals and places?
3. What can people do to save wild animals and places?
4. What would the world be like without wild animals and places? Do you think it will happen someday? Why or why not?
5. If you could spend your life working for a cause, what would it be? Why do you think that cause is important?

The Jouberts speak at the National Geographic Society, 2006.

Reading 2

Pre-Reading

Preparing for the Reading Topic

A Discuss these questions with your classmates.

1. Why is it difficult for girls and women to get an education in some countries?
2. How can education change a person's future?
3. What are the schools like for the children in your hometown? Are they modern or traditional?
4. What did you like about school when you were a child? What didn't you like?

B Imagine you are someone who wants to do something that goes against your family and cultural traditions. Which of the following characteristics would you need to have? Check two. Then explain why.

_____ a strong will

_____ bravery

_____ cleverness

_____ toughness

Key Vocabulary

As you read "Educating Kenya's Girls", pay attention to the following words and see if you can work out their meanings from the context.

remote	brave
loyal	honors
optimistic	opportunities
tribe	forced
expected	confident

Kakenya Ntaiya

Unit 4 People Making a Difference 77

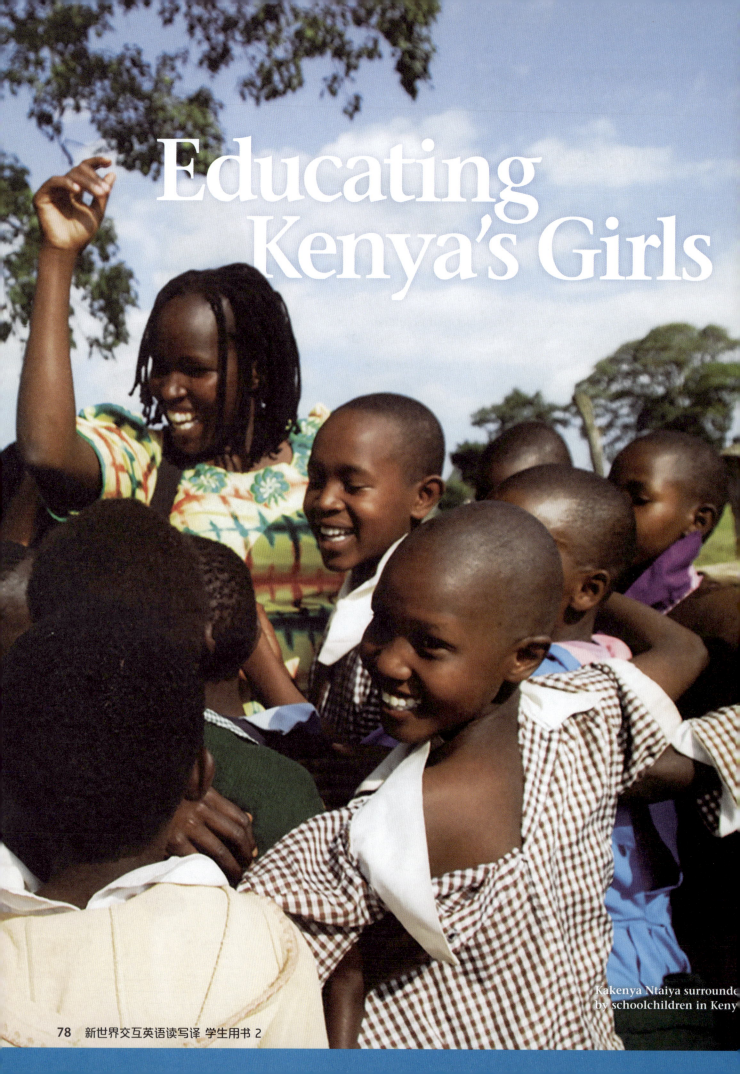

Educating Kenya's Girls

Kakenya Ntaiya surrounded by schoolchildren in Kenya

1   In the **remote** Kenyan[1] village of Enoosaen, there is a school where there was never one before, and over 150 girls are now getting an education. The woman who built this school was from this village. But she was also very different. She was courageous, determined, **loyal**, and **optimistic**. Her name is Kakenya Ntaiya.

2   Ntaiya is the oldest of eight children in her family, belonging to Kenya's Maasai[2] **tribe**. When Ntaiya was young, her father worked in a distant city, and the family was extremely poor. They lived in a grass and mud hut that they shared with goats and sheep. They had no electricity. As the eldest, Ntaiya helped to feed and care for the younger children. She carried water, gathered firewood, cooked meals, and worked in the field. Like all the girls in her village, she was supposed to follow tradition and learn the skills to be a good Maasai wife.

3   At the age of five, Ntaiya's father engaged her to a six-year-old neighbor. Her father **expected** her to marry at age 13, as was the custom. Ntaiya's mother wasn't happy. She wanted more for her children. But there was little she could do to help them. She, too, had to follow tradition. However, Ntaiya didn't feel the same way. She had a plan. And she was **brave** enough to make it work.

4   Ntaiya loved going to school. She made excellent grades and even dreamed of being a teacher herself one day. Few girls dared to have dreams like that. Even today, only 11 percent of girls from Ntaiya's village continue their education past primary school. Instead, at age 13, a Maasai girl marries and begins to have children of her own. However, Ntaiya didn't want to marry or go through the ceremonies for a girl of that age. With all the courage she could find in herself, she went to her father. She told him she would run away if she had to stop her education. She said she would do what he wanted if he let her finish high school. Her father agreed. Ntaiya graduated from high school with top **honors**.

5   After graduation, Ntaiya decided she wanted to attend college—a university in the United States. By then, however, her father was sick and in a hospital. All the family money went to his care, so there was no money for Ntaiya. Ntaiya had once been brave enough to go against tradition, her father, and the village leaders. Now she had to do it again. She was determined to follow her dreams.

6   At first the leaders were against Ntaiya. They were angry with her for daring to do what even few boys dreamed about. She promised she would use her education to help the village. She promised to come back and build a school. One village leader saw her determination and agreed to help her. The village gave her money, and she also received a scholarship to Randolph-Macon[3] Women's College in the United States. In 2004, Ntaiya received her bachelor's degree. Later, she got a job at the United Nations[4]. In 2011, she received her doctorate in education—all made possible by her courage and her will to succeed.

7   Ntaiya did not forget her promise to the village. Loyal to her people and her beliefs, she returned to Enoosaen. In 2009, she opened the first primary school for girls in her village, the Kakenya Center for Excellence. The school has been a great success. There

---

1 Kenyan 肯尼亚的
2 Maasai 马赛，部落
3 Randolph-Macon 兰道尔夫麦肯学院
4 the United Nations 联合国

the students have education and **opportunities** that Ntaiya had to fight so hard for. Girls that were once **forced** to marry at 13 are now dreaming of becoming doctors, lawyers, pilots, and business women.

8   Ntaiya knows that change comes slowly and is difficult. But she is optimistic about the future. As a girl, she had dreams and was **confident** that her dreams were possible. Today, she sees the positive changes in her students and their families. She believes that the future for the women of Kenya, and of other countries too, can change through education, one girl at a time. Ntaiya is looking forward to building more schools—always hopeful, always determined.

Vocabulary

A Complete these sentences with the words in the box.

brave	expected	honors	opportunities	remote
confident	forced	loyal	optimistic	tribe

1. A group of people who have the same race, language, and customs, and who live together in the same area is a(n) _____.

2. _____ are chances or conditions that allow you to do something.

3. Something is _____ when people believe that someone will do something, or something will happen, in the usual and normal way.

4. A(n) _____ person believes in his or her ability to do something.

5. A(n) _____ area is far away and apart from other places.

6. You are _____ when you deal with danger, pain, or difficult situations with courage.

7. A person who is _____ believes that what happens will be good and that things will end well.

8. When people are _____ to do something, it means that someone or something makes them do it even if they don't want to.

9. A(n) _____ person is faithful and tells the truth to one's family, group, or country.

10. _____ are awards or recognition given to people for achieving high marks in their course work.

B Answer these questions with complete sentences.

1. What homework assignments are you **expected** to do this week?

2. What is something you are **confident** that you can do?

3. What **opportunities** would you like to have in your life?

4. What is a **remote** place in the country you come from?

5. What are you sometimes **forced** to do that you don't really want to do?

C Now write your own sentences. Use the following words in the sentences: **honors**, **optimistic**, **loyal**, **tribe**, and **brave**.

Reading Comprehension

A Circle the letter of the best answer.

1. Which of the following best expresses the main idea of this passage?
    a. It is difficult for some girls to get an education.
    b. Ntaiya's courage and determination helped her achieve her dream.
    c. Traditions and customs are an important part of life.
    d. Attitudes toward women and girls are changing around the world.

2. What was Ntaiya's life like when she was a child?
    a. She worked hard to help her family survive.
    b. She was unable to go to school.
    c. She lived a better life than most of the people in her village.
    d. She wanted to follow the customs of her tribe.

3. Which one did Ntaiya not do to help the family when she was a girl?
    a. Worked in a distant city.
    b. Carried water.
    c. Gathered firewood.
    d. Cooked meals.

4. How did Ntaiya prove she was a loyal member of her tribe?

   a. She studied hard at her college in the United States.

   b. She dreamed about having a better life.

   c. She understood the importance of education for everyone.

   d. She fulfilled her promise to return and help the village.

5. Why is Ntaiya optimistic about the future of the girls in her village?

   a. They could earn more money than ever before.

   b. They live a better life by following Ntaiya's dream.

   c. They have opportunities for education and careers.

   d. They stopped marrying for an early age.

B Choose the correct word/phrase from the box to complete each of the following sentences according to the reading passage.

| A. courageous | B. get engaged | C. determination | D. supposed | E. share |

1. I have some very sad news to _____ with all of you.

2. He was wrong, but _____ enough to admit it.

3. Yuri shows great _____ to learn English.

4. Jack will _____ to Ann next month.

5. We're _____ to check out of the hotel by 11 o'clock.

Critical Thinking

Discuss these questions with your classmates.

1. Do you think following tradition is important? Why or why not?

2. What are some traditions you would like to change in your culture or family? Why?

3. How can educated people make a difference in a village, a country, or in the world?

4. What do you think is a good age for men and women to marry? Do you think parents should tell their children when and whom to marry? Why or why not?

5. Are attitudes towards women and girls changing in the world today? Why or why not?

Writing

Writing Skills

The Descriptive Essay

Often when we write a *descriptive essay*, we use the dominant impression. The *dominant impression* is the main effect a person, place, or thing has on our feelings or senses.

- We give the dominant impression by selecting the most important feature or character trait of a person, place, or thing and emphasizing it. Adjectives like **shy**, **dedicated**, **determined**, or **generous** can easily give a dominant impression. This impression is then supported by details.

- The first topic sentence in a paragraph will usually give you the dominant impression.

    EXAMPLES: As well as being **dedicated**, the Jouberts are **daring**.
    The Jouberts are not only a **patient** couple, but they are a **passionate** one as well.

Exercise 1

Look at each dominant impression and the group of sentences below it. In each case, find the sentences that do *not* support the dominant impression. Circle the answers.

1. My brother is *ambitious*.
    a. He likes to watch the latest news on television.
    b. He takes extra classes at school.
    c. He's captain of his football team.
    d. He's already decided that he wants to be a doctor.
    e. He takes a trip to Switzerland every year.

2. My best friend is *shy*.
    a. She never speaks to people at a party.
    b. She likes to read books a lot.
    c. She never raises her voice.
    d. She likes to wear green sweaters.
    e. She always disappears when I want to introduce her to someone.

3. My aunt is *kind*.
    a. She always remembers my birthday.
    b. She likes to work in the garden.
    c. She likes to listen to classical music and read poetry.
    d. She always offers me a cup of tea when I visit.
    e. She offers me a sweater when I'm cold.

Exercise 2

Read the following essay written by a student. Then answer the questions at the end of the essay.

My Cousin Patricia

My cousin Patricia is a teacher who works for Santa Maria de Fatima High School in Peru. She has been teaching there for the last six years. She is 32, but she looks much younger. Patricia is a very nice person to get along with and has some very good qualities.

Patricia believes all people are equal. She likes to show people that women as well as men can do everything and be successful. When she talks about current events, she likes to mention the achievements of men and women of all races and nations. She often asks her students to do research on organizations in which people work together to make the world a better place.

My cousin is a good leader. If you ever had a chance to join any of her group meetings, you would notice right away how she enjoys leading others while encouraging them to participate in what is going on. When there are decisions to be made, she listens to everyone's opinions and respects everyone's suggestions. People who know that trait of her like her very much. People like to be with her, and she has many friends. The only bad thing I can say about her is that I don't see her often enough.

In conclusion, my cousin Patricia is very nice in many ways, is a very good teacher, and is the best company a person could have. I wish she didn't live so far away, but someday maybe she will come to live near my family. That will be a wonderful day.

1. Where is the thesis statement? Circle it.
2. What is the topic sentence in each of the body paragraphs? Underline it.
3. In the topic sentence of each body paragraph, double underline the words that give you the dominant impression.

The Narrative Essay

A *narrative* tells a story of events or actions. A narrative puts events in time and tells us what happened according to a natural time sequence. A narrative is also a description of people and places. The story of Kakenya Ntaiya is a narrative essay.

- Here are some examples of time-order words and phrases that are used to show the order in which events happen.

a few days later	finally	meanwhile	then
after, afterward	first (second, etc.)	next	when
after a while	for the next [number] years	one day	
eventually	in 2011	soon	

- Time-order words and phrases at the beginning of a sentence are followed by a comma.

    EXAMPLE: After graduation, Ntaiya decided she wanted to attend college.

- Here are some examples of descriptions from the Kakenya Ntaiya's story.

    EXAMPLES: She was confident that her dreams were possible.
    She was courageous, determined, and optimistic.
    She is optimistic about the future.

- We use adjectives to describe people and places. Adjectives modify nouns. They come before nouns, but they come after some verbs like be, become, and get.

    EXAMPLES: She was <u>confident</u> that her dreams were possible.
                           adjective
    She was <u>courageous</u>, <u>determined</u>, and <u>optimistic</u>.
                   adjective   adjective   adjective
    Her father worked in a <u>distant</u> <u>city</u>.
                                            adjective noun

Exercise 3

These sentences about Kakenya Ntaiya are not in the correct time order. Number the sentences in the correct time order. The first one is done for you.

_____ 1. Ntaiya receives a scholarship to a U.S. college.

_____ 2. Ntaiya tells her father she will run away unless she can finish high school.

_____ 3. Ntaiya decides she wants to attend college.

_____ 4. Ntaiya gets a job at the United Nations.

_____ 5. Ntaiya builds the Kakenya Center for Excellence.

__1__ 6. Ntaiya's father engages her to a six-year-old neighbor.

_____ 7. A village leader agrees to help Ntaiya.

_____ 8. Ntaiya receives her doctorate in education.

_____ 9. Ntaiya graduates from high school with top honors.

_____ 10. Ntaiya dreams of being a teacher one day.

_____ 11. Ntaiya receives her bachelor's degree.

Exercise 4

Complete the paragraph about Ntaiya's life with the words in the box.

| after that | difficult | later | poor | determined | in 2009 |
| courageous | in 2004 | loyal | remote | optimistic | when |

Ntaiya was born in a(n) 1._____ village in Kenya. Her family was 2._____. 3._____ she was five, her father engaged her to her six-year-old neighbor. Ntaiya was expected to marry at age 13, but she didn't want to. She wanted to go to school. She was a(n) 4._____ girl and asked her father to let her finish high school. Her father agreed. After she graduated, she wanted to go to college in the United States, but there was no money for her to go. A village leader agreed to help her because she was 5._____. The village gave her money, and Ntaiya received a scholarship to a U.S. college. 6._____, Ntaiya received her bachelor's degree. 7._____, Ntaiya got a job at the United Nations. Ntaiya was 8._____ to her people and returned to her village. 9._____, she opened the Kakenya Center for Excellence. 10._____, Ntaiya received her doctorate in education. Ntaiya knows that change is 11._____, but she is 12._____ about the future.

Ntaiya speaks at The American Natural History Museum, New York, U.S.A., November 2013.

Writing Practice

Write an Essay

Choose one of the following topics to write a narrative essay.

1. The story of your life
2. The life of a person you know
3. The life of a famous person
4. The person who influences your life

Pre-Write

A Work with a partner and brainstorm events in the person's life and descriptions about the person.

B Make a list of your events and descriptions and work on a thesis statement for your essay.

Outline

Fill in the outline below. Write your thesis statement, and arrange the events from Exercise B in Pre-Write in the correct order, in two or more body paragraphs. Finally, write your conclusion.

Essay Outline

Introduction

Thesis statement: _____

_____

_____

Body Paragraph 1

Topic sentence: _____

_____

_____

   Supporting detail 1: _____

   Supporting detail 2: _____

Body Paragraph 2

Topic sentence: _____

_____

_____

   Supporting detail 1: _____

   Supporting detail 2: _____

Body Paragraph 3

Topic sentence: _____

_____

_____

   Supporting detail 1: _____

   Supporting detail 2: _____

Conclusion

Restatement of thesis: _____

_____

_____

Final comment: _____

Write and Revise Your Essay

Translation

A Translate the following passage into English.

大熊猫是一种温顺的动物，它长着独特的黑白皮毛，是熊科动物中最稀有的成员。大熊猫被誉为"中国国宝"，主要生活在中国西南部的森林里。这些以竹为食的动物正面临许多威胁，因此，确保大熊猫的生存十分重要。大熊猫对于世界自然基金会（WWF）有着特殊意义。自1961年该基金会成立以来，大熊猫就一直是它的徽标。

B Translate the following passage into Chinese.

In order to promote equality in education, China has invested 36 billion yuan for the improvement of the educational facilities in rural areas and the enhancement of rural compulsory education in the mid-west. The fund is used to improve teaching facilities and to purchase books, benefiting more than 160,000 primary and middle schools. Meanwhile, the fund is used to provide musical instruments and painting supplies. Nowadays, like the children in coastal cities, those living in rural and mountain areas also have music and painting lessons. As a result, some students, who would have transferred to cities for better education, remain in the local schools now.

Weaving It Together

Unit Project

In this part, you are required to do some research among your classmates, friends or relatives. Collect information about saving wildlife. Then give a presentation to your classmates. The following questions can be used as references.

1. Why is the world losing wild animals and places?
2. What are endangered species?
3. What are the threats to animals and wildlife?
4. What can we do to protect wildlife?
5. Why should we protect wildlife?

Searching the Internet

A Search the Internet for information about these animal conservationists: Willie Smits, Alan Rabinowitz, Ric O'Barry, and Eugenie Clark. Find answers to these questions:

1. Where were they born?
2. What animal(s) is/are their main focus?
3. Where are these animals found?

B Search the Internet for three countries with the lowest literacy rates and find the literacy rates for women in these countries. Share the information with your classmates.

What Do You Think Now?

Refer to Page 69 at the beginning of this unit. Do you know the answers now? Circle the best answer.

1. Africa (is/isn't) losing its wild places and animals.
2. It (is/isn't) easy to photograph wild animals.
3. Girls (can/can't) go to school everywhere in the world.
4. It (is/isn't) possible for one woman to build a school.

Broadening Your Horizon

A

Things You Can Do To Protect Wildlife

It is often easy to feel overwhelmed by the loss of species and habitat destruction. The problem is serious and complex—it's common for individuals to feel powerless. Yet, everything we do is vitally important. We may only do a little bit in the grand scheme of things, but together our seemingly small actions add up to a lot.

B

Top 10 Most Endangered Animals in China

More and more animals in China have been classified as endangered species because of the effects of natural disasters and human activities. Most of the endangered species can be found only at reserves. The key to save endangered animals is to provide a safe environment to them.

C

Why Protect Wildlife?

America's wildlife enriches the nation in a multitude of ways. Many of us enjoy recreational activities that depend on wildlife or wildlife habitat. In 2001, for example, 34 million Americans went fishing; 13 million hunted; and over a third (66 million) watched or photographed wildlife.

UNIT 5
Food

At a weekend market in Oaxaca, Mexico, traditional Oaxacan dishes are on sale for lunch.

WHAT DO YOU THINK?

Answer these questions with your best guess. Circle *Yes* or *No*.

1. Does sushi mean "raw fish"? Yes   No
2. Are American sushi and Japanese sushi the same? Yes   No
3. Do people all over the world typically have a small breakfast? Yes   No
4. Is a continental breakfast small and sweet? Yes   No

Reading 1

Pre-Reading

Preparing for the Reading Topic

A Discuss these questions with your classmates.

1. Do you like to eat sushi? Why or why not?

2. Are there restaurants in your city that serve food from other countries? If so, what kind of foods do they serve? Are any of them your favorite restaurant?

3. Do you think food in foreign restaurants is the same as that served in the restaurant's native country? Why or why not?

B Which descriptions do you associate with American sushi, Japanese sushi, or both? Fill in the chart below. Write the letters of the descriptions from the list under the types of sushi. Then after you have read "Sushi Crosses the Pacific", review your answers.

a. spicy
b. small servings
c. white rice
d. large servings
e. made with avocado
f. raw fish
g. rolled inside out
h. served in a beautiful design
i. not a lot of spices or toppings

American Sushi	Japanese Sushi	Both Types of Sushi

A sushi chef in a sushi restaurant in Las Vegas, Nevada, U.S.A. shows off one of his dishes.

Key Vocabulary

As you read "Sushi Crosses the Pacific", pay attention to the following words and see if you can work out their meanings from the context.

borders   order
suit   recommends
ingredient   accompanied
seasonings   servings
appealed   stir

Sushi Crosses the Pacific

1   Once, people only ate food from other countries by traveling to them. But today it's common to eat Indian food in London, Mexican food in New York, and Chinese food in Denmark. But is the person in Denmark eating the same food as the person in Beijing? Probably not. Something happens to food when it crosses **borders**. People change it to **suit** their tastes. A good example is when sushi[1] made the journey across the Pacific and landed in Los Angeles.

2   People often think sushi means raw fish. Raw fish is the most popular **ingredient** in sushi, but the main ingredient is rice. The term sushi refers to the rice, which has

---
1 sushi 日本寿司

special **seasonings**. Any food made with this seasoned rice can be called sushi. Sushi first started in Southeast Asia and then became popular in Japan where the Japanese made it an art form. Today, sushi has become popular around the world.

3   After the 1970s, sushi became especially popular in the United States. It all started in Little Tokyo in Los Angeles, where a Japanese chef created the California roll. He didn't invent it for Americans but for his Japanese customers. Because he couldn't always find the right tuna, he decided to use avocados, of which California has plenty. Later, sushi spread beyond Little Tokyo and **appealed** to Americans. Today there are thousands of sushi bars, restaurants, and take-out shops across the United States. Is American sushi the same as Japanese sushi? Not quite. There are similarities and differences, especially in the way people **order**, eat, and make sushi.

4   In many sushi bars and restaurants in the United States and Japan, there are menus for customers to select from, or they can ask the chef or waiter what he or she **recommends**, or customers can ask for certain things they like. Both countries use conveyor belts in some sushi bars, which makes it much easier to order. Small plates of sushi ride around on the belt, and customers pick the dishes they want to try.

5   There are also similarities in the way sushi is eaten and prepared. In both countries, people eat sushi with their fingers or with chopsticks. Similarly, sushi is presented beautifully on plates, with careful attention to design and color. Also, the sushi is **accompanied** by soy sauce, pickled ginger, or a green, spicy paste called wasabi[2]. In both countries, white rice is usually used for sushi and is seasoned with salt, vinegar, and sugar. Likewise, the rice is mass-produced for speed and ease. The rice is mixed with sweetened vinegar in factories and delivered to supermarkets, hotels, and take-outs shops. In better restaurants in both countries, sushi chefs cook and season their own rice. Similarly, they use fresh, raw fish.

6   In as many ways as sushi is the same in the two countries, there are also differences. Many Americans don't know how to order sushi, so they order only what they see on the menu, while more Japanese ask the chef to make them special dishes they like. Many Americans often order several **servings** of similar items. In contrast, most Japanese customers order different plates because variety is important to them.

7   There are also differences in the way sushi is eaten. In Japan, chefs put a small amount of wasabi in the nigiri[3] between the rice and topping. But many Americans like spicy food, so they want wasabi on the side in order to **stir** it

2 wasabi 芥末酱
3 nigiri 握寿司

into the soy sauce and put this all over the fish. However, this is never done in Japan, because it's important to taste the fish. Also, Americans dip the rice side of the nigiri into soy sauce, whereas Japanese dip the fish side. Many Americans eat the pickled ginger while they are eating their sushi. But for the Japanese, pickled ginger is there to cleanse the palate between servings.

8   Probably the biggest difference is in the way sushi is prepared. Many Americans prefer sushi rolls rather than nigiri. And the rolls are made inside out, with the rice on the outside! Moreover, the sushi rice is a little sweeter and the servings are much larger than in Japan. And Americans have added things like cream cheese, spicy mayonnaise, and deep-fried seafood. Compare that with traditional nigiri: a piece of fresh fish, a tiny piece of wasabi, and some pure white rice.

9   Sushi has come a long way from Japan. Today sushi has traveled back to Japan in the form of American sushi, where the Japanese can experience this foreign food.

Vocabulary

Vocabulary in Context

A Complete these sentences with the words in the box.

| accompanied | borders | order | seasonings | stir |
| appealed | ingredient | recommends | servings | suit |

1. A(n) _____ is one of the things from which a type of food is made.
2. When someone _____ something, that person advises or suggests it to someone else.
3. Something that _____ to you, pleased you.
4. _____ are portions of food offered to people for eating.
5. When you _____ a meal, you ask for certain food to be brought to you.
6. _____ are put on food to give it a special taste.
7. _____ are the dividing lines between countries.
8. Something is _____ when something else is with it at the same time.
9. To _____ is to satisfy or please.
10. To _____ is to mix something by moving a spoon around in it.

B Answer these questions with complete sentences.

1. What is one **ingredient** in sushi?

2. What are the names of two countries that share a **border**?

3. What dessert would you **recommend** to a friend?

4. What color **appeals** to you?

5. What kind of weather **suits** you?

C Now write your own sentences. Use the following words in the sentences: ***accompanied***, ***servings***, ***stir***, ***order***, and ***seasonings***.

Vocabulary Building

Complete these sentences with the correct form of the **bold** words. You may use your dictionary.

1. recommend
   a. We went to the sushi bar on a friend's _____.
   b. I _____ a book for my brother to read on the train.

2. accompany
   a. Rain often _____ wind during a storm.
   b. That music is the perfect _____ for his singing voice.

3. seasoning
   a. As I was _____ the potatoes, the top of the spice bottle came off.
   b. I forgot to _____ the salad, so it was quite plain.

Reading Comprehension

A Circle the letter of the best answer.

1. When did sushi start to appeal to Americans?
   a. When its ingredients were made simpler.
   b. When they saw it could be mass-produced.
   c. After ingredients they like were added.
   d. From the first day it was made in Los Angeles.

2. What are the two main similarities between American and Japanese sushi?
   a. The spiciness of the sushi and the use of chopsticks.
   b. The seasoned white rice and fish and the beautiful presentation.
   c. The way the sushi is dipped and how it is prepared.
   d. The use of conveyor belts and mass-produced rice.

3. What are the two main differences between American and Japanese sushi?
   a. The way it is ordered and presented.

b. How it's made in factories and the types of spices added.

c. What the restaurants look like and how they recommend plates.

d. How it is prepared and the way it is eaten.

4. Why did many Americans order only what they see on the menu?

   a. Because it is relatively easier and more convenient.

   b. Because they have no idea about how to order sushi.

   c. Because they have no other choice.

   d. Because it is the habit.

5. Why did the Japanese chef who created the California roll use avocados?

   a. Because California has plenty.

   b. Because avocados taste better than tuna.

   c. Because it's the customers' wishes.

   d. Because the Japanese chef wanted to be more creative.

B Each statement below contains information given in the passage. Identify the paragraph from which the information is derived.

1. Both America and Japan use conveyor belts, which makes it much easier to choose. Paragraph _____

2. Many Americans love sushi rolls better than nigiri. Paragraph _____

3. The love of variety is the reason why most Japanese customers order different plates. Paragraph _____

4. The popularity of sushi among Americans began in Los Angeles. Paragraph _____

5. The rice is mass-produced for speed and ease. Paragraph _____

6. Many Americans eat the pickled ginger with their sushi. Paragraph _____

7. Any food made with seasoned rice can be called sushi. Paragraph _____

8. When sushi travels back to Japan, the Japanese can experience this foreign food. Paragraph _____

Critical Thinking

Discuss these questions with your classmates.

1. Do you like to try foods from other countries? Why or why not? What are some foods that you absolutely would not eat? Why?

2. What is your favorite food from your country? What is your favorite food from another country?

3. What parts of American culture do you like? What parts don't you like? Why?

4. Is food and eating meals important in your culture? Why or why not?

5. Do you think presentation (how the food looks on the plate) is important? Why or why not?

Reading 2

Pre-Reading

Preparing for the Reading Topic

A Discuss these questions with your classmates.

1. What do you eat for breakfast?
2. What are the most popular breakfast foods in China?
3. What are some popular breakfast foods around the world?

B Match the breakfasts with the countries. Then after you have read "What's for Breakfast?", check your answers.

_____ 1. Bacon, eggs, toast, marmalade

_____ 2. Coffee, bread, pastries

_____ 3. Same as lunch or dinner

_____ 4. Tortillas, eggs, coffee

a. France
b. Mexico
c. England
d. China

Key Vocabulary

As you read "What's for Breakfast?", pay attention to the following words and phrase and see if you can work out their meanings from the context.

pastries	items
substantial	grab
inevitably	rush off
savor	reflect
skip	distinct

Cooking in sub-zero conditions on a mountain in Queen Maud Land, Antarctica

What's for Breakfast?

1   What's for breakfast? Depending on where you live, you might start your day with boiled eggs or pancakes, rice or cereal, fish or **pastries**. Your breakfast might be large or small, and it might be sweet, spicy, or salty. From Bulgaria to Buenos Aires, breakfasts differ in size, taste, and ingredients. They are as varied as the cultures on our planet.

2   Some countries have **substantial** breakfasts, whereas others like them small. Northern and Eastern Europeans, who live in cold climates, often like to start their

day with a large, hot breakfast. Many Russians eat sausages, fried eggs, and a variety of breads. Similarly, Germans, Austrians, and Scandinavians generally prepare a generous meal that includes cereal, eggs, breads with butter and jam, cold meats, cheeses, yogurt, and fruits. They drink coffee, tea, milk, or hot chocolate with all these foods. Likewise, the English, Scottish, and Irish love a full breakfast when they have the time. Their plates are heavy with bacon, sausages, a variety of egg dishes, grilled tomatoes, mushrooms, and **inevitably** toast with marmalade or jam. On the other hand, a small or "continental" breakfast of coffee and bread or pastries suits people who go to cafés in places like France, Italy, Belgium, and Greece.

3   Not only is the continental breakfast small, but it is also sweet, in contrast with the salty breakfast enjoyed in some countries. While some Europeans **savor** their sweet pastries, many Middle Easterners prefer a saltier breakfast that includes beans with olive oil and lemon juice. Also, in countries like Greece and Turkey, a popular breakfast item is feta[1] cheese as well as olives.

4   Many Mexicans and Central Americans like to start the day with a spicy meal. Mexico's most common food ingredient is the chili pepper, and Mexicans see no reason to **skip** their favorite spice at breakfast. A spicy sausage called chorizo, as well as eggs and breakfast burritos (fresh tortillas spread with beans, eggs, cheese, and chopped meat) served with hot sauces, are commonly enjoyed with several cups of coffee. Like the Mexicans, the Central Americans enjoy their spicy breakfasts. Their egg dishes, sausages, and fried plantains are all flavored with a variety of peppery seasonings.

5   Does breakfast have to be different? Although many countries have special breakfast foods, some countries treat breakfast the same as any other meal. Take China for instance. The Chinese eat rice, vegetables, and meat in the morning as well as for lunch and dinner. Just as in China, breakfast in Japan is no different from other meals and often includes miso soup, rice, vegetables, seaweed, and fish. Likewise, in Southeast Asia and Malaysia, morning foods look like any other meal. Rice, noodles, curries, beans, and soups are all popular **items** on the breakfast table—or the vendor's cart, as the case may be.

6   In today's world of globalization, people are less likely to follow tradition than they did in the past. Japanese youth are more likely to eat fried eggs and ham than their parents' steamed rice. Germans are eating more American-style breakfast cereals. Swedes may **grab** a container of yogurt or a sandwich before they **rush off** for work. In West Africa, the citizens of former French colonies favor continental breakfasts, while many East Africans enjoy larger English-style breakfasts. Fast foods are becoming more common everywhere, however, and **reflect** the pace of modern life. Nevertheless, there are still **distinct** differences among cultures. A traveler can still enjoy the pleasure of having some chicken soup and rice and beans in Colombia and Peru, or the thin rice pancakes called *appam* in India, or Vietnam's *xoi*, which is sticky rice steamed in a leaf. Variety is, after all, the spice of life, and the richness of tradition is a joy to experience— or in this case, to eat.

---

1 feta 羊乳酪

Vocabulary

A What are the meanings of the **bold** words? Circle the letter of the best answer.

1. Depending on where you live, you might start your day with eggs, cereal, fish, or **pastries**.
   - a. cakes made from rice
   - b. large, flour-based breads
   - c. white, salty crackers
   - d. sweet cakes made with flour

2. Some countries have **substantial** breakfasts.
   - a. large
   - b. average
   - c. tiny
   - d. unusual

3. While some Europeans **savor** their sweet pastries, Middle Easterners prefer a saltier breakfast.
   - a. eat all of
   - b. enjoy the taste of
   - c. save part of
   - d. make a meal of

4. Mexicans see no reason to **skip** their favorite spice at breakfast.
   - a. jump over
   - b. use up
   - c. include
   - d. leave out

5. People in the United Kingdom can have a full breakfast with eggs but **inevitably** have toast.
   - a. without doubt
   - b. surprisingly
   - c. strangely
   - d. finally

6. Popular **items** on the breakfast table include beans and soups.
   - a. points
   - b. things
   - c. ideas
   - d. moments

7. Swedes **grab** a sandwich before they go to work.
   - a. eat
   - b. catch
   - c. quickly obtain
   - d. enjoy

8. Swedes quickly buy a container of yogurt and then **rush off**.
   - a. eat it up
   - b. finish it up
   - c. slow down
   - d. hurry away

9. Fast foods **reflect** our modern life.
   - a. warn
   - b. cut
   - c. mirror
   - d. simplify

10. There are still **distinct** differences among cultures.
    - a. difficult to understand
    - b. clearly seen
    - c. commonly known
    - d. largely unknown

B Answer these questions with complete sentences.

1. What are some **pastries** you like to eat?

2. What do you consider to be a **substantial** breakfast?

3. Why do some people **skip** breakfast?

4. What is a popular food **item** people sell on the streets?

5. What is a food you **grab** when you don't have any time?

C Now write your own sentences. Use the following words in the sentences: **savor**, **inevitably**, **rush off**, **reflect**, and **distinct**.

Reading Comprehension

A Circle the letter of the best answer.

1. What is the main idea of the reading passage?
   a. Modern life is affecting the way people eat around the world.
   b. There are similarities and differences in breakfast foods around the globe.
   c. Some countries like hot foods for breakfast while others don't.
   d. Although breakfast foods are popular, some countries eat the same type of food all day.

2. What is the main idea of the first paragraph?
   a. People eat differently depending on where they live.
   b. People eat various foods for breakfast.
   c. Breakfast choices.
   d. Some people enjoy a large breakfast while some prefer a small one.

3. What is the main topic of the second paragraph?
   a. The type and amount of breakfast foods differ among regions.
   b. People who live in cold climates like large, hot meals at breakfast.
   c. The French and Italians like to eat what is known as a "continental" breakfast.
   d. Germans and Scandinavians like large breakfasts with breads, meats and eggs.

4. What is the main idea of the fourth paragraph?
   a. Mexicans are addicted to spicy food.
   b. Central Americans love spicy breakfast.
   c. Mexicans and Central Americans like a spicy meal at the start of the day.
   d. Mexicans and Central Americans are used to eating spicy breakfast.

5. What is the main idea of the sixth paragraph?
   a. The Germans and Swedes are starting to eat smaller breakfasts.
   b. Fast food is becoming more popular for breakfast around the world.
   c. Breakfast traditions are changing in the modern world.
   d. There are many places where people still eat traditional foods.

B Choose the best answer to each question or to complete each statement.

1. People from which countries like spicy breakfast?
   a. Mexicans and Italians.
   b. Japanese and Central Americans.
   c. Japanese and Mexicans.
   d. Mexicans and Central Americans.

2. Because of _____ , people are less likely to follow tradition than before.
   a. globalization
   b. advances in technology
   c. convenient transportation
   d. the Internet

3. Who generally prepares a generous meal?
   a. Germans and Austrians.
   b. Austrians and Scandinavians.
   c. Germans and Scandinavians.
   d. Germans, Austrians, and Scandinavians.

4. What is a continental breakfast like?
   a. Generous and sweet.
   b. Small and salty.
   c. Small and sweet.
   d. Generous and salty.

Critical Thinking

Discuss these questions with your classmates.

1. What are your favorite breakfast foods?
2. Do you prefer a large breakfast or a small breakfast? Explain why.
3. Does the younger generation in your country eat a different breakfast than the older generation? Explain why.
4. Do you think your eating habits are healthy? Explain why.
5. How has modern life changed the general eating habits of people around the world? Do you think that is good or bad? Explain why.

Writing

Writing Skills

Comparison and Contrast Words and Phrases

It is important to use the correct *comparison and contrast words and phrases* to introduce your points. The following table contains a list of some words and phrases.

- **Comparison Words and Phrases**

Sentence Connectors	Clause Connectors	Others
similarly likewise also	as just as and	like (+ noun) similar to (+ noun) just like (+ noun) (be) similar to (be) the same as both... and not only... but also

- **Contrast Words and Phrases**

Sentence Connectors	Clause Connectors	Others
however nevertheless in contrast on the other hand on the contrary	although even though while whereas	but yet despite (+ noun) in spite of (+ noun) (be) different from

Exercise 1

Read the following essay written by a student. Then answer the questions at the end of the essay.

Food Customs in Iran

Food customs around the world are strongly connected to culture, tradition, and geography. We can see this in my country, Iran. It has a variable climate, which gives us the advantage of having a large variety of foods to eat. However, what we eat is still influenced by our traditions and geography, as we can see in the similarities and differences between the north and south of Iran.

Many of the food customs are similar everywhere in the country. For example, in both Northern and Southern Iran, food is eaten with one's hand and a piece of bread instead of using utensils. Rice is an important staple in Iran, and it is a part of almost every meal in both the north and the south. Another similarity between the north and south is eating fish, since both areas are near seas: the Caspian Sea in the north and the Persian Gulf in the south.

caviar

    Because the north of Iran is quite different from the south, there are several differences in eating habits between the two areas. Northern Iran faces the Caspian Sea, where we find the special fish from which the famous caviar is made and that northerners love to eat. Because of the Mediterranean climate in the north, rice is one of the major crops, and it plays an important role at the table in Northern Iran. Rice is served at all ceremonies. As a tradition, northerners conduct a rice ceremony every year by putting rice twigs in the paddy and singing songs. In Southern Iran, which faces the Persian Gulf, the favorite dishes include a wide variety of seafood—especially the whitefish. Although rice is important and a part of most meals, the south is better known for its vegetables and fruits. Dates, in particular, are important and are a major export to Western countries.

    In conclusion, Iran is a large country with a diverse geography and people. As in all large countries, a variety of customs can be found on all points of the compass. Food customs in particular are influenced by climate and location, making Iran a very interesting country in which to live and eat!

1. Where is the thesis statement for the whole essay? Circle it.
2. What are the topic sentences in each of the body paragraphs? Underline them.
3. What are the points of similarity? What are the points of contrast?
4. Circle the comparison and contrast words and phrases used by the student.
5. Does the essay have a concluding sentence? Where is it? Is it a restatement of the thesis statement, or a summary of the main points and a final comment?

Using *while* and *whereas*

While and *whereas* have the same meaning and are both used in the same way. Both words are used to show that something is in contrast to or directly the opposite of something else. They can be used at the beginning or in the middle of a sentence.

- *While* and *whereas* can be used with either of the elements you are comparing with no change in meaning. Note the use of commas below with *while* and *whereas*.

    EXAMPLES: The meat is sweet, **whereas** the vegetables are salty.
    The meat is sweet, **while** the vegetables are salty.
    While the vegetables are salty, the meat is sweet.
    Whereas the vegetables are salty, the meat is sweet.

Exercise 2

Combine the two sentences into one using **while** or **whereas** at the beginning of the sentence. Use correct punctuation.

1. California grows lots of avocados. Avocados are not widely found in Japan.

2. Most Japanese eat sushi. Many Americans won't eat raw fish.

3. Sushi rolls are in every American sushi bar. In Japan, nigiri is the most popular sushi dish.

4. Japanese want their sushi simple and fresh. Many Americans like to add ingredients such as vegetables and spices.

5. Japanese sushi chefs study for years. Many American sushi chefs have only a few months of training.

Using *although*, *even though*, and *though*

Although, *even though*, and *though* all have the same meaning. They introduce an adverbial clause that shows a contrast or an unexpected idea. These clauses are useful when you are comparing and contrasting something. Use a comma when the adverbial clause begins a sentence.

EXAMPLES: **Although** many countries have special breakfast foods**,** some countries treat breakfast like any other meal.

Some countries treat breakfast like any other meal **although** many countries have special breakfast foods.

Even though many countries have special breakfast foods**,** some countries treat breakfast like any other meal.

Some countries treat breakfast like any other mean **even though** many countries have special breakfast foods.

Though many countries have special breakfast foods**,** some countries treat breakfast like any other meal.

Some countries treat breakfast like any other meal **though** many countries have special breakfast foods.

Exercise 3

Combine the two sentences into one by using *although* or *even though*. Use the correct punctuation.

1. The English muffin sounds like it comes from England. It is actually an American invention.

2. Breakfast in Central America commonly includes eggs, sausages, and plantains. The South American breakfast is more like the light "continental" breakfast of France and Italy.

3. Some Russians like coffee for breakfast. Most Russians enjoy an early cup of strong, hot tea.

4. Breakfast foods are different among various countries across the continent. Fresh fruit is popular at breakfast in most parts of Africa.

5. Eggs, potatoes, and curries are commonly eaten at breakfast in India. Breakfast in Kashmir to the north is just tea and bread.

6. People drink tea throughout the day in China. They don't often drink tea at meals.

Writing Practice

Write an Essay

Choose one of the following topics to write a comparison-and-contrast essay.

1. The way people serve and eat food in the United States and in another country
2. The behavior expected from a guest or host in the United States and in another country
3. Eating at a restaurant in the United States and in another country
4. Two fast-food restaurants in the same country

Pre-Write

A Work with a partner and brainstorm examples of the similarities and differences of your topic.

B Make a list of your examples, and work on a thesis statement for your essay.

Outline

Fill in the outline below. Write your thesis statement, and pick the two or three best points of comparison and contrast from Exercise B in Pre-Write. Finally, write your conclusion.

Essay Outline

Introduction

Thesis statement: _____

_____

Body Paragraph 1

Topic sentence: (point 1) _____

_____

    Similarities: _____

    Differences: _____

Body Paragraph 2

Topic sentence: (point 2) _____

_____

    Similarities: _____

    Differences: _____

Conclusion

Restatement of thesis: _____

_____

Final comment: _____

Write and Revise Your Essay

Translation

A Translate the following passage into English.

在西方人心目中，和中国联系最为密切的基本食物是大米。长期以来，大米在中国人的饮食中占据着很重要的地位，以至于有谚语说"巧妇难为无米之炊"。中国南方大多种植水稻，人们通常以大米为食；而华北大部分地区因为过于寒冷或过于干燥，无法种植水稻，那里的主要农作物是小麦。在中国，有些人用面粉做面包，但大多数人用面粉做馒头和面条。

B Translate the following passage into Chinese.

Breakfast may not be the most important meal of the day, but eating a healthy breakfast has been shown to lower the risk of Type 2 diabetes in adults and to lower the risk of heart disease in men. According to an observational study in 2014, eating a healthy breakfast has helped to reduce weight and maintain a healthy weight. Many studies have linked eating breakfast to good health. It's hard to know, though, if having breakfast creates these healthy habits or if people who eat it already have healthier lifestyles.

Weaving It Together

Unit Project

In this part, you are required to do some research among your classmates, friends or relatives. Collect information about food. Then give a presentation to your classmates. The following questions can be used as references.

1. What do you think is the relation between food and culture?
2. What is your understanding of the saying, "Hunger is the best appetite"?
3. What is the most popular fast-food in China?
4. Is breakfast as important as the other meals in China?

Searching the Internet

A Search the Internet for information about four kinds of flatbread from around the world: tortilla, pita, injera, and lavash. Find answers to these questions:

1. Where is it eaten?
2. What is it made of?
3. How and when is it eaten?

B Search the Internet for interesting facts about how people drink coffee and tea in different countries around the world. Share the information with your classmates.

What Do You Think Now?

Refer to Page 93 at the beginning of this unit. Do you know the answers now? Complete the sentence, or circle the best answer.

1. Sushi means _____.
2. American sushi and Japanese sushi (are/are not) the same.
3. People all over the world typically (have/do not have) a small breakfast.
4. A continental breakfast (is/is not) small and sweet.

Broadening Your Horizon

 A

10 Facts You May Not Know About Eating in China

Different countries have different eating customs. This article will help you to know the basic facts about eating in China.

B

U.S. Food

For our next series, Maps of World will be exploring the cuisine of the United States. We'll take a peek into kitchens across the country in an attempt to define exactly what constitutes American cuisine. Food is at the heart (and stomach) of every culture, and as we take a closer look at the culinary specialties around the country, it becomes clear that the food we eat is a reflection of who we are and where we've been. As a nation formed of immigrants from varied backgrounds, the food of the United States closely resembles the history of its people.

C

Hawaii Food

Hawaii is home to a unique blend of people and cultures, including the early Polynesians who have inhabited the islands for many years, European explorers, and later immigrants from China, Japan, Korea, the Philippines, Portugal, and the rest of the United States. As a series of islands in the middle of the Pacific Ocean, Hawaii has been relative isolation for many years, which has allowed the culture of the islands to develop and evolve over its history. The culture and cuisine that have been created are vastly different from that of the mainland, as they call the rest of the United States, characterized by a relaxed lifestyle with food playing a central role.

Unit 5 Food   113

UNIT 6 Language

Chinese characters carved into stone in Zhangjiakou, China

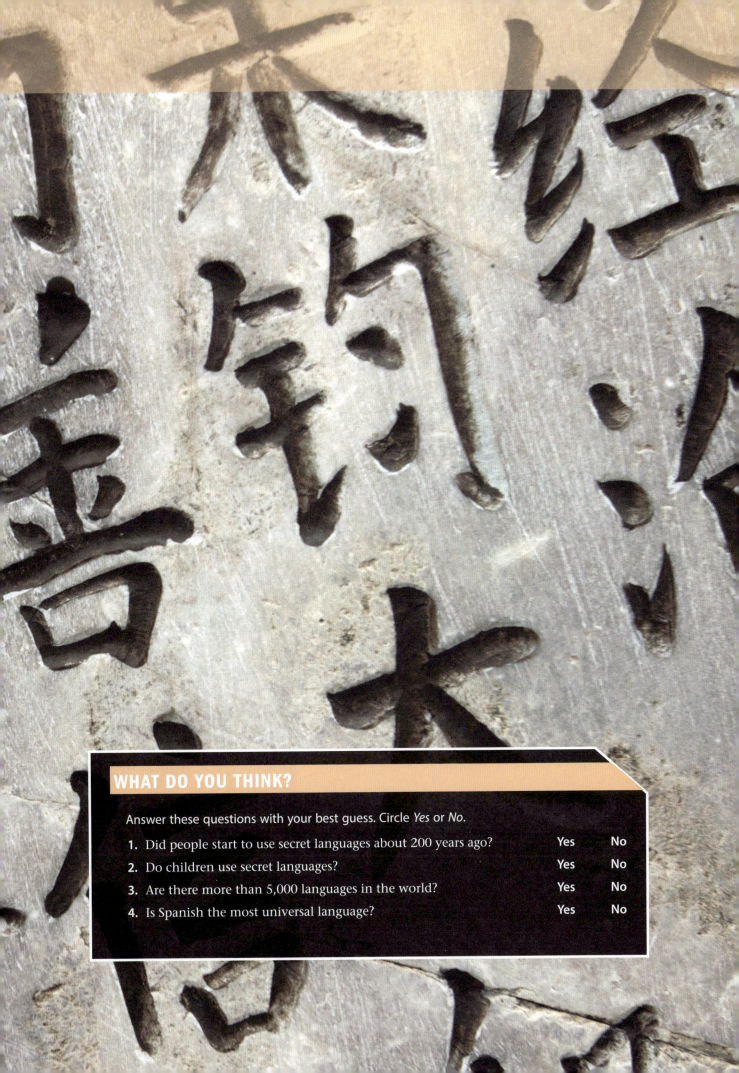

WHAT DO YOU THINK?

Answer these questions with your best guess. Circle *Yes* or *No*.

1. Did people start to use secret languages about 200 years ago?   Yes   No
2. Do children use secret languages?   Yes   No
3. Are there more than 5,000 languages in the world?   Yes   No
4. Is Spanish the most universal language?   Yes   No

Reading 1

Pre-Reading

Preparing for the Reading Topic

A Discuss these questions with your classmates.

1. Did you ever make up a secret language as a child? If so, how and why did you use it?

2. What are secret codes, and how are they used by spies or in war time?

3. Do you know any abbreviations used in texting? How can it be helpful to know these abbreviations or codes?

B Answer these questions. Then after you have read "Keeping It Secret", check your answers.

1. In text messaging, what do you think the following items mean?

   BRB   BTW   GMTA   LOL   TTYL

2. Why do you think texting is popular among teens?

Key Vocabulary

As you read "Keeping It Secret", pay attention to the following words and phrases and see if you can work out their meanings from the context.

invisible	transmit
dipped in	undecipherable
reliable	cracked the code
substituting	intercept
decoded	devices

A boy whispers into a young girl's ear in Nowy Tag, Poland.

Keeping It Secret

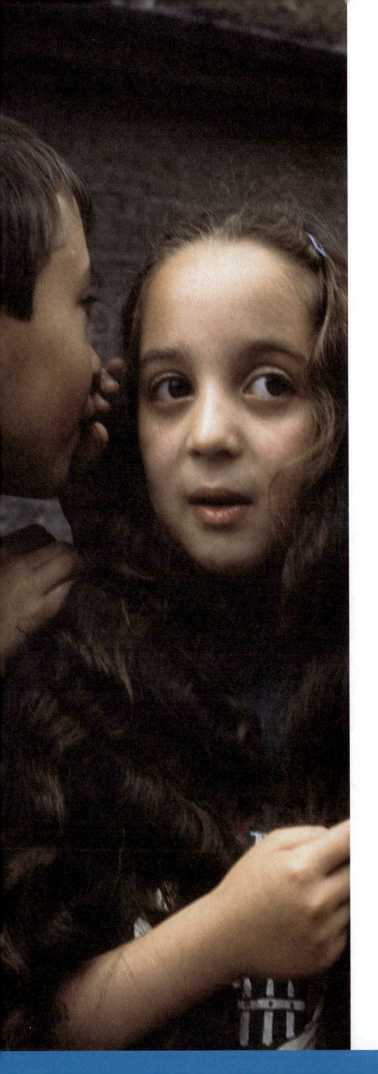

1   There's a saying that secret languages are for children, lovers, and spies. But they are also for governments, businesses, workers, and criminals, among others. They can be a matter of fun or survival. There are many types, causes, and uses of secret languages. However, they all have these two characteristics in common: they are understood by only a select group, and they are meant to keep information from others.

2   There are many ways of keeping communication secret. One way is to make words **invisible**. This can be done by writing with a pen **dipped in** any number of elements, such as lemon juice or vinegar. The words disappear once the paper dries. Putting heat near the paper makes the lemon juice letters show up again. Spray the vinegar message with red cabbage water and the writing turns purple! A more **reliable** way to write a message in secret is to develop a code. Codes have existed since the beginning of recorded history. They're made by **substituting** letters, numbers, or symbols for letters or whole words, or by mixing the letters in a word. Both methods make words incomprehensible to anyone who doesn't know the code.

3   Codes have many uses, both amusing and important. Children have always enjoyed creating their own language to keep secrets. The most popular and well-known language is Pig Latin, which is formed by

moving the first letter to the end of the word and adding "ay" to it. For example, "Mary had a little lamb" becomes "Arymay adhay aay ittlelay amblay". But codes often have more vital uses, particularly when used by the military. In war, the making and breaking of codes have caused both victory and defeat. In World War II, the British developed a machine that successfully **decoded** German messages. Because the British were able to learn about German military plans, the Germans lost the war.

4   The Americans also used secret codes during the war. The Marines in the Pacific used Navajo[1] "code talkers" to **transmit** messages. Because the Japanese were expert code solvers, the U.S. military needed an **undecipherable** code. The native Americans of the Navajo tribe had a complex, unwritten language understood by few outsiders. Navajo soldiers in the U.S. military developed their own code talk. For example, the Navajo word for hummingbird[2], *dah-he-tih-hi*, meant "fighter plane". Sometimes the first letters of Navajo words spelled a message. The Japanese never **cracked the** Navajo **code**. Military officers have said the United States would have lost the Battle of Iwo Jima[3] without the code talkers.

5   Government spies and soldiers aren't the only ones who want to keep communications secret. Codes are used by many different people and groups. Businesses

---
1 Navajo 纳瓦霍人，美国最大的印第安部落
2 hummingbird 蜂鸣鸟
3 Iwo Jima 硫磺岛，位于北太平洋日本以南

Native American members of the Navajo Code Talkers, shown here in Washington, D.C., in 2012

need codes to protect their ideas or processes. As a result, workers in a common profession often have a secret language to keep information private, or they use it simply as a way to easily communicate among themselves. And criminals have always made use of secret languages. Imagine having the police **intercept** your plans to rob a bank.

6   Secrecy isn't the only purpose for codes. Today's technologies have driven the creation of a new type of code language for sending text and instant messages. Known as Web lingo or Webspeak, it's a type of shorthand that allows quick communication via cell phones and other electronic **devices**. Some examples include writing BRB when one will "be right back" and LOL when one is "laughing out loud". Among teenagers, Webspeak has also become a way of hiding information from parents. POS means "parent over shoulder", and KPC means "keeping parents clueless". Not for long, though. As parents know that too many secrets can be dangerous, they're quickly learning the rules of Webspeak to understand their teens' new language.

7   Secret languages can be games children play or ways to keep a country safe. They can aid criminals or save lives. The important thing about secret languages is that they play a vital role in how humans use language in their lives. There will always be a need and desire for these languages—and for the creativity it takes to make and use them.

Vocabulary

Vocabulary in Context

A What are the meanings of the **bold** words? Circle the letter of the best answer.

1. One way of keeping communications secret is to make words **invisible**.
   - a. unable to be seen
   - b. unable to be heard
   - c. made useful
   - d. known only by a few

2. Keeping communications secret can be done by writing with a pen **dipped in** any number of elements.
   - a. dropped into a liquid
   - b. sprayed with a liquid
   - c. quickly put in and out of a liquid
   - d. held down into a liquid

3. Codes may be made by **substituting** letters, numbers, or symbols.
   - a. breaking
   - b. replacing
   - c. developing
   - d. creating

4. The British developed a machine that successfully **decoded** German messages.
   - a. broke into smaller parts
   - b. sent back
   - c. discovered the meaning of
   - d. made use of

5. Writing words that disappear is not a **reliable** way to send a secret message.
   - a. continual
   - b. regular
   - c. dependable
   - d. hard

6. The Marines in the Pacific used Navajo "code talkers" to **transmit** messages.
   - a. create
   - b. send
   - c. hide
   - d. discover

7. The U.S. military needed an **undecipherable** code.
   - a. easily understood
   - b. impossible to read
   - c. difficult to create
   - d. unable to be sent

8. The Japanese never **cracked the code**.
   - a. discovered the meaning of
   - b. received all the pieces of
   - c. made a new language from
   - d. destroyed the meaning of

9. Imagine having the police **intercept** your plans to rob a bank.
   - a. stop
   - b. break apart
   - c. make a copy of
   - d. throw away

10. Webspeak allows quick communication via cell phones and other electronic **devices**.
    - a. projects
    - b. tools
    - c. plans
    - d. ideas

B Answer these questions with complete sentences.

1. What is a common disease people **transmit**?
   _____
   _____

2. What is an electronic **device** you use every day?
   _____
   _____

3. What food tastes better after it is **dipped in** a sauce?
   _____
   _____

4. What can you **substitute** for butter?
   _____
   _____

5. Who is the most **reliable** person in your family?
   _____
   _____

C Now write your own sentences. Use the following words in the sentences: *invisible*, *decoded*, *undecipherable*, *cracked the code*, and *intercept*.

_____
_____
_____
_____
_____

Vocabulary Building

Complete these sentences with the correct form of the **bold** words. You may use your dictionary.

1. **reliable**
   a. He's never late so you can _____ on him to be on time.
   b. Don't expect too much from her because she's not a _____ person.

2. **substitute**
   a. Our teacher was absent so we had a _____ teacher instead.
   b. The _____ of yogurt in place of fat works well in some recipes.

3. **transmit**
   a. There's a live _____ of the car chase on television.
   b. The satellite _____ data to Earth.

Reading Comprehension

A Circle the letter of the best answer.

1. Which of the following is NOT the characteristic of secret languages?
    a. The purpose of secret languages is to hide messages from outsiders.
    b. Secret languages are written with pen dipped in vinegar.
    c. There are a variety of types, causes and uses of secret languages.
    d. Only a certain group of people can understand secret languages.

2. What's the main idea of the second paragraph?
    a. There are many reasons why people need to keep communications secret.
    b. Codes have existed for centuries.
    c. There are several methods of making writing disappear.
    d. There are various ways to keep communications secret.

3. Why does the author give the example of Pig Latin created by children?
    a. To show that children's secret language is of no importance.
    b. To show the amusing creativity of children.
    c. To show some uses of codes are to amuse people.
    d. To show Latin is very difficult to learn.

4. Web lingo is created due to _____.
    a. the need to communicate quickly via electronic devices
    b. the need to hide information from parents
    c. the need to know children's secrets
    d. the need to create a new type of secret language

5. What is the main idea of this passage?
    a. Secret languages are used by a variety of people.
    b. Keeping communication secret is the main purpose of secret languages.
    c. Military officers need to learn about their enemy's secret languages to win.
    d. There are many types, causes and uses of secret languages.

B Each statement below contains information given in the passage. Identify the paragraph from which the information is derived.

1. A code played an important role in the Battle of Iwo Jima.   Paragraph _____
2. Secret languages have a promising future.   Paragraph _____
3. Secret languages are used in a variety of organizations, groups and professions.   Paragraph _____
4. Technologies play an important role in creating new types of code language.   Paragraph _____
5. Codes are used to keep secrets by children.   Paragraph _____
6. Lemon juice and vinegar are used to keep communication secret.   Paragraph _____

Critical Thinking

Discuss these questions with your classmates.

1. Have you ever learned or used a secret language? If so, how and why? If not, would you like to? Why?
2. If you could make up your own secret code, how would you do it? When, where, how, and why would you use it?
3. Do you know any common Web lingo words and abbreviations? What do they mean?
4. Young people use Webspeak to keep secrets from their parents. What are the positive and negative effects of this? Do you think teens and adults have always struggled to communicate? Why or why not?
5. In what ways are secret languages good? In what ways are they bad?

Reading 2

Pre-Reading

Preparing for the Reading Topic

A Discuss these questions with your classmates.

1. Describe the photo on Pages 124–125. What country do you think it is?

2. In your hometown, what English words do you see on the streets, in shops, and in restaurants?

3. Why do people like to use these English words?

B Answer these questions. Then after you have read "English Around the World", check your answers.

1. The following words are all taken from English and used in other languages. What do you think the original English words are?

   herkot   rushawa   sueter   mi ke fung

2. Why do you think other languages borrow words from English?

Key Vocabulary

As you read "English Around the World", pay attention to the following words and phrase and see if you can work out their meanings from the context.

universal	concern
borrowed	disappearing
threatening	inevitable
fines	preserving
eliminate	pop up

People ride an elephant past a road sign in English and Cambodian in Siem Reap, Cambodia.

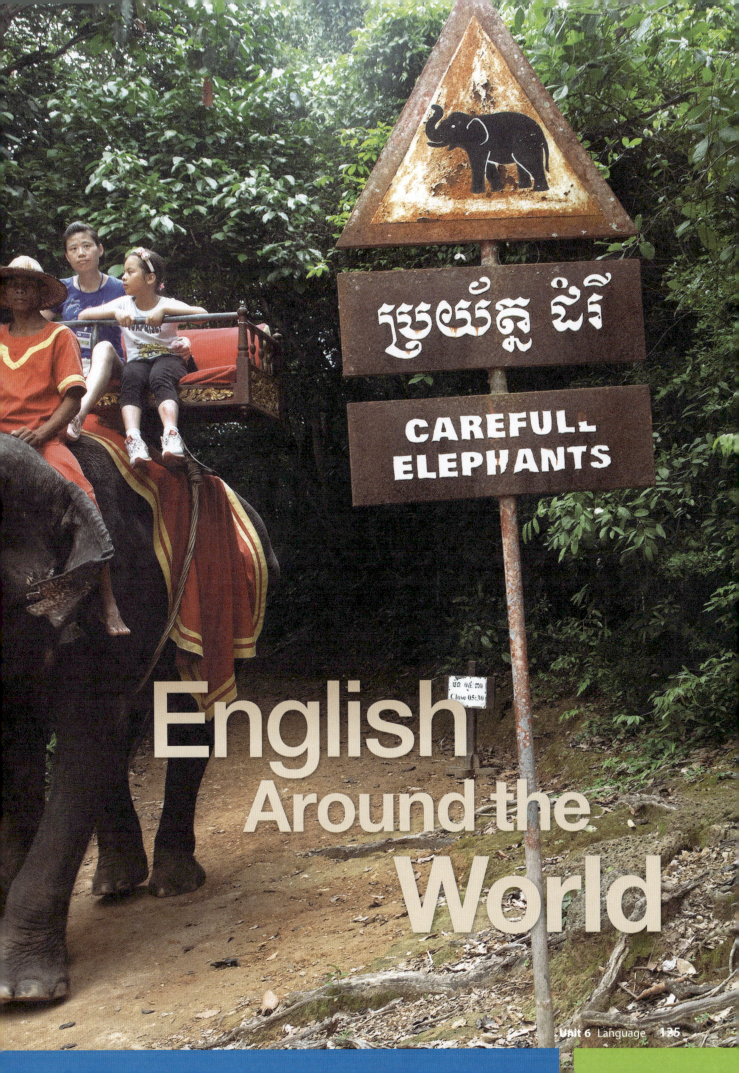

English Around the World

1   Do you speak English? That question is frequently asked in countries around the world. Although there are over 6,000 languages, English is the most **universal**. It is the official language in over 50 countries and the most used language in international business, science, and medicine.

2   Even in countries where English is not the first language, a number of English words are used. No other language is **borrowed** from more often than English. For example, a French worker looks forward to *le weekend*. A Romanian shopper catches a ride on the *trolleybus*. A Chinese singer sings on the *mi ke fung* (microphone). Some Swedish[1] schoolgirls have even started making the plural forms of words by adding -s, as in English, instead of the Swedish way of adding -ar, -or, or -er.

3   Hundreds of words borrowed from English can now be found in other languages. Some of these words are soda, hotel, golf, tennis, jeans, OK, baseball, and airport. Although many words are used just as they are, others are changed to make them more like the native language and therefore easier to say and remember. Thus, a Japanese worker gets stuck in *rushawa* (rush-hour) traffic. A Spanish mother tells her child to put on her *sueter* (sweater), and a Ukrainian[2] man goes to the barber for a *herkot* (haircut).

4   English is everywhere. It is on signs, clothing, soft drinks, and household products around the world. In spite of the popularity of English words and phrases, however, they are not always welcome. Some people think that the use of English words is **threatening** the purity of their native language. In 1975, the French started a commission to try to stop, and even give **fines** for, the use of English words. Some countries have tried to **eliminate** English as their official language in order to save their native tongue.

5   On the other hand, some people believe that English should be the international language. They give a number of reasons for this, such as the cost of translations and the misunderstandings that result from language differences. They believe that things would run more smoothly if everyone spoke the same language.

6   "What would become of our many different cultures?" others argue. "Certainly the world would be a much less interesting place," they add. Indeed, among language experts there is serious **concern** that many languages are **disappearing**. In some parts of the world, only a few people are left who can speak the native tongue. In Ireland, for example, there are only a few small areas where people speak Irish Gaelic[3], the native Irish language. One expert says that half of the world's languages are dying because children are no longer learning them.

7   Languages have changed and disappeared throughout history. With progress, change is **inevitable**. Some things are worth **preserving**. Others are not. The difficulty is in deciding what is worth keeping. Because people have very strong feelings about the importance of their native language, we probably will not have a universal language in the near future. One thing is certain, however: English words will continue to **pop up** everywhere, from Taiwan to Timbuktu[4], whether some people like it or not.

---

1 Swedish 瑞典的
2 Ukrainian 乌克兰的
3 Gaelic 盖尔语
4 Timbuktu 廷巴克图，常用来指偏远的地方

Vocabulary

A Complete these sentences with the words or phrases in the box.

borrowed	disappearing	fines	pop up	threatening
concern	eliminate	inevitable	preserving	universal

1. _____ are money you have to pay as a punishment.
2. Something concerning everyone in the world is _____.
3. A(n) _____ is a feeling of worry about something important.
4. Something that will definitely happen is _____.
5. Something that is becoming impossible to see or find is _____.
6. To _____ is to appear suddenly and unexpectedly.
7. _____ something is keeping it from being damaged or harmed.
8. To _____ is to get rid of something completely.
9. When things or words are taken from somewhere and copied, they are _____.
10. If something is likely to harm or destroy something, it is _____ it.

B Answer these questions with complete sentences.

1. What is something you pay a **fine** for?

2. What is something you **borrow** at school?

3. What is a **concern** for most parents?

4. What would be **inevitable** if you did not study for your exam?

5. What is one English word you think is **universal**?

C Now write your own sentences. Use the following words in the sentences: *disappear*, *eliminate*, *pop up*, *preserving*, and *threatening*.

Unit 6 Language 127

Reading Comprehension

A Circle the letter of the best answer.

1. Which of the following best expresses the main idea of this passage?
   a. English and its influences on other languages around the world.
   b. Many languages borrow words from English.
   c. English will become a world language.
   d. People should preserve dying languages.

2. Why do many countries want to stop the use of English words?
   a. Because they want to fine people who use English words.
   b. Because they want to eliminate English as their official language.
   c. Because English words and phrases are very popular in those countries.
   d. Because they believe that English language is damaging the purity of their native languages.

3. Which of the following is NOT one of the reasons given by those who believe that English should be the international language?
   a. It can save the cost of translations.
   b. Other languages are not as important as English.
   c. There will be fewer misunderstandings caused by language differences.
   d. Things would run more smoothly if everyone spoke the same language.

4. What is the main idea of the sixth paragraph?
   a. Some people's objection against the idea of English being the universal language.
   b. Language experts' concern about disappearing languages.
   c. Only a small number of people speak the native Irish language.
   d. Many languages are dying because children are no longer learning them.

5. What is the author certain about?
   a. Some languages will disappear.
   b. English is worth preserving.
   c. English words will still be used around the world.
   d. We will have a universal language in the near future.

B Match each of the sentences in Column A with the words from Column B.

Column A

1. _____ is borrowed the most often.
2. _____ is mentioned that tried to give fines for the use of English words.
3. Some people believe that things would run more _____ if everyone spoke the same language.
4. Some language experts are concerned that many languages in the world are _____.
5. English will continue to _____ in the near future.

Column B

a. successfully
b. appear unexpectedly
c. France
d. English
e. dying

Critical Thinking

Discuss these questions with your classmates.

1. Why have languages disappeared throughout history?
2. How would you stop a language from dying out?
3. Do you think all languages must be preserved? Why or why not?
4. Why do you think English has become a global language?
5. What language other than English would be a good candidate as a global language? Why?

Unit 6 · Language 129

Writing

Writing Skills

Writing about Reasons

An essay that discusses *reasons*, answers the question Why? You look at a situation and write the reasons for that situation. Usually there is more than one reason for a situation. It is important to look at all the reasons. When there are many reasons, there is usually one that is the most important.

- In an essay that lists reasons, the thesis statement tells the reader what the situation is and that there are reasons for this situation or reasons for doing something about this situation.

- Each of the body paragraphs gives a reason and supports it with good examples.

- Often writers state the most important reason last. This will make your essay more interesting. If you state your most important reason first, the reader will not have anything to look forward to.

Introducing Reasons with *because* and *as*

Because and *as* are transitions that introduce a reason clause. They answer the question Why? Both *because* and *as* can be used at the beginning or in the middle of a sentence.

EXAMPLES: Children have always enjoyed creating their own languages as / because
they love to keep secrets.

Because / As children love to keep secrets, they have always enjoyed creating their own languages.

- Use a comma after the reason if you start the sentence with *because* or *as*.

Exercise 1

Combine the two sentences into one using **as**. Combine three of the sentences with **as** in the middle and another three of the sentences with **as** at the beginning.

1. Businesses need to keep information private. They use a secret language or code.

2. The Germans lost the war. The British decoded German messages.

3. Pig Latin is easy to form. Children use it to keep secrets.

4. The Navajo language was complex and unwritten. Few outsiders were able to understand it.

5. The U.S. military needed an undecipherable code. The Japanese were experts at codes.

6. Teenagers use Webspeak. Teenagers want to keep secrets from their parents.

Exercise 2

Read the following essay written by a student. Then answer the questions at the end of the essay.

Learning English Is Important to Me

When I first came to the United States of America, I found out the importance of knowing English. Whenever I went to the market to buy food, to the post office to mail a letter, or to take a bus to the bank, I had to communicate in English or things would not go smoothly. But the two most important reasons for learning English for me are to be able to go through the interview process to get a job and to be able to read English to know what is going on in the world.

First, learning English is essential if I wish to go through the interview process to get a job. It is important to feel comfortable with the language and be able to converse without hesitation with the interviewer. Even if the interview is in another language, sometimes the interviewer will switch to English just to test your fluency. But conversation is not enough; I must be able to understand formal written English, including contracts. When I was in Hong Kong, I went for an interview and was given a letter of employment to read and sign. The letter stated, "You will have a nine-month probation period, and one month's notice or payment in lieu of notice has to be given if either party wants to terminate the contract during the probation period." I did not know what "payment in lieu of" or "terminate" meant. I could not ask the interviewer or I would not get the job. I signed the contract and started the job. I quit six months later without prior notice. Because I did not understand the contract, I lost a month's salary.

Second, learning English is important for me because I want to know what is going on around me in the world. When I read newspapers and magazines in my own language, I feel I am not getting enough news of the world. I believe that Western reporters communicate all kinds of news in greater detail, and this will give me a different perspective. Also, being able to read magazines and newspapers in English will

> keep me aware of the technological changes that will be affecting us all. With recent advances in technology, the world is changing rapidly in many fields, such as business, arts, and medicine. These changes will affect me soon, and it is important for me to read and keep up with these changes.
>
> In conclusion, it is important for me to learn English so that I will feel confident about myself when I go for a job interview again. It is also important as I want to know what is happening in the world around me, and by learning English I can do this. In fact, learning English is the answer to a lot of the things that I need and want.

1. What is the thesis statement for the whole essay? Circle it.
2. What are the topic sentences in each of the body paragraphs? Underline them.
3. How many reasons does the student give for the importance of learning English?
4. What transitions are used to introduce reasons? Double underline them.

Words That Signal Cause and Effect

Certain words and phrases signal a cause or an effect. Here are some that you may already know.

- Words that signal a cause—the reason for something:

    The first reason…   *The next cause…*   *Because…*

    EXAMPLE: **Because** children are no longer learning the native tongues of their grandparents…

- Words that signal an effect—the result:

    The first effect…   *As a result,…*   *Consequently,…*

    EXAMPLE: **Consequently**, many languages are disappearing.

Exercise 3

Decide if the following statements in each pair are a **C** (*Cause*) or **E** (*Effect*).

1. a. Half of the world's languages are dying. _____
   b. Children no longer learn them. _____
2. a. The Umutina tribal language of South America disappeared. _____
   b. The only person who spoke the language died in 1988. _____
3. a. Children in France are not learning the Breton language in schools. _____
   b. The Breton language in France is near extinction. _____
4. a. The Amish, a religious group in America, have kept their language, Pennsylvania Dutch, alive for three centuries. _____
   b. They speak Pennsylvania Dutch at home. _____
   c. They do not have telephones or television. _____

> ### Using *therefore* and *consequently*
>
> ***Therefore*** and ***consequently*** are sentence connectors. They connect two clauses when the second clause is the result of the first clause. ***Consequently*** and ***therefore*** have the same meaning as the coordinator *so*.
>
> EXAMPLES: <u>English is the most universal language</u>; **consequently** / **therefore**, <u>it is the language
> cause
> most used for science, medicine, and business.</u>
> effect
>
> - Use a semicolon before and a comma after ***consequently*** and ***therefore***.

Exercise 4

Read the pairs of sentences. Underline the clause that gives the effect. Then combine the two sentences, adding **therefore** or **consequently** before the effect clause. Use the correct punctuation.

1. Sometimes English words are changed to make them more like the native language. English words are easier to say and remember.

   _____
   _____

2. In France, where English is not spoken, many words are borrowed. A French worker looks forward to *le weekend*.

   _____
   _____

3. English words are becoming popular in other languages. Some people are afraid that the purity of their language is threatened.

   _____
   _____

4. There will be no universal language in the near future. People have strong feelings about the importance of their language.

   _____
   _____

Writing Practice

Write an Essay

Choose one of the following topics to write a cause-and-effect essay.

1. The causes and effects of having English as a global language
2. The effects English (in American music, food, sports, etc.) has had on your language and culture
3. The effects the English language and culture have had on you

Pre-Write

A Work with a partner and brainstorm examples for your topic.

B Make a list of your examples, and work on a thesis statement for your essay.

Outline

Fill in the outline below. Write your thesis statement for the topic of your essay, and pick the two best examples from Exercise B in Pre-Write for the topics of your body paragraphs. Finally, write your conclusion.

Essay Outline

Introduction

Thesis statement: _____

_____

_____

Body Paragraph 1

Topic sentence: _____

_____

_____

    Supporting detail 1: _____

    Supporting detail 2: _____

Body Paragraph 2

Topic sentence: _____

_____

_____

    Supporting detail 1: _____

    Supporting detail 2: _____

Conclusion

Restatement of thesis: _____

_____

_____

Final comment: _____

Write and Revise Your Essay

Translation

A Translate the following passage into English.

复杂的汉字（Chinese characters）书写体系是中国古代文化传承下来的瑰宝，而这一体系正面临着退化的命运。随着电脑和智能手机的迅速发展和普及，年轻人提笔忘字的现象越来越常见。若不借助电子产品的帮助，很多人难以写出1万个常用字。为此，中央电视台开播了一档汉字听写比赛（Chinese Character Dictation Competition）节目，以引起人们对汉字的重视，帮助观众提高汉字书写能力。

B Translate the following passage into Chinese.

Though how the English language came into existence remains a mystery to many people, linguists believe that English and most other European languages have descended from a common source: the Indo-European parent language. English was first spoken by the Anglo-Saxons who invaded England in the fifth century. They passed onto us the basic vocabulary of English. In over fifteen centuries of its development, English has enriched itself by massive borrowing. As British immigrants landed in America and established the United States as an independent nation, a new variety was added to the English language: American English. Though some people worry that the language is running out of control, many native speakers of English take pride in the tolerance of their language.

Weaving It Together

Unit Project

In this part, you are required to do some research among your classmates, friends or relatives. Collect information about their attitudes towards Web lingo words. Then give a presentation to your classmates. The following questions can be used as references.

1. Do they know some Web lingo words as well as their meanings? Give some examples.
2. Are there any Web lingo words that have become a part of our formal languages? Give some examples.
3. Can Web lingo words do good to native languages? Why or why not?
4. What can we do to keep Web lingo words from harming both native speakers and native languages?
5. Do they believe some Web lingo words should be preserved? Why or why not?

Searching the Internet

A Search the Internet for information about words in English that are borrowed from other languages. Find two words from each of these languages that are used in English:

1. French _____ _____
2. Italian _____ _____
3. Russian _____ _____
4. German _____ _____
5. Japanese _____ _____
6. Spanish _____ _____

B Search the Internet for the latest Webspeak words and their meanings. Share the information with your classmates.

What Do You Think Now?

Refer to Page 115 at the beginning of this unit. Do you know the answers now? Complete the sentence, or circle the best answer.

1. People started using secret languages _____.
2. Children (use/don't use) secret languages.
3. There are over _____ languages in the world.
4. _____ is the most universal language.

Broadening Your Horizon

A

Are Dying Languages Worth Saving?

Language experts are gathering at a university in the U.K. to discuss saving the world's endangered languages. But is it worth keeping alive dialects that are sometimes only spoken by a handful of people? You may find the answer in the passage.

B

Chinese Language "Damaged by Invasion of English Words"

The "invasion" of English words into the Chinese language must be stopped or it will no longer be a pure language, according to the country's most senior translator.

C

The Secret Language

Do you desire to create your own secret language? This passage introduces the fundamental rules and several simple ways of creating secret languages.

UNIT 7 Environment

Aerial view of farmland in Wisconsin, U.S.A.

WHAT DO YOU THINK?

Answer these questions with your best guess. Circle *Yes* or *No*.

1. Do zoos exist only to entertain people? Yes No
2. Can animals get a condition called zoochosis from being in a zoo? Yes No
3. Does the United States grow the most genetically modified crops? Yes No
4. Are genetically modified crops more nutritious? Yes No

Reading 1

Pre-Reading

Preparing for the Reading Topic

A Discuss these questions with your classmates.

1. What zoos do you know of, and how are the animals kept in them?
2. Why do we keep animals in zoos?
3. Do you think animals are happy in zoos?

B Answer these questions. Then after you have read "Behind Bars at the Zoo", check your answers.

1. What are the reasons for keeping animals in zoos? Make a list.
2. How is each of the following words connected with the topic of zoos?

   breed   control   conserve

   confine   capture   educate

Key Vocabulary

As you read "Behind Bars at the Zoo", pay attention to the following words and phrases and see if you can work out their meanings from the context.

was founded	endangered species
confined	database
conserve	extinct
dignity	instinct
pacing up and down	adapt

Giraffes at Cheyenne Mountain Zoo in Colorado Springs, Colorado, U.S.A.

Behind Bars at the Zoo

1   It was in 1826 that the Zoological Society[1] **was founded** in London. In 1847, the word *zoo* was first used. Later on, in 1892, the Englishman Henry Salt[2], in his book *Animals' Rights*[3], was one of the first to protest against keeping animals in cages. He did not like the way the animals were **confined** in cages and the way animals in zoos lose their "character". Since then, many people have criticized zoos for these reasons. However, zoos claim that their role is to educate the public and **conserve** animals. These aims are not bad in themselves. It is the way in which they are carried out that we

---

1 Zoological Society 动物学会
2 Henry Salt 亨利·萨尔特
3 *Animals' Rights* 《动物的权利》

must consider.

2 Zoos claim that they have an important educational function. Is this true? In reality, most people go to zoos for entertainment. This is what sells the tickets and pays the bills. Zoos say they give people the opportunity to see the wonders of nature and its wild animals. In fact, they are showing us animals that have lost their **dignity**: animals with sad and empty eyes. The conditions under which animals are kept in zoos change their behavior. Animals, like humans, are affected by their environment.

3 After months and years in a cage, animals begin to lose their natural characteristics. Many animals in zoos get signs of zoochosis[4], abnormal behavior, which includes endlessly **pacing up and down** and rocking from side to side. It is caused by lack of space, lack of company, lack of enrichment, and an unsuitable diet. Two polar bears in the Bristol[5] Zoo in England were confined in a small area for 28 years and showed all the signs of zoochosis. How can people observe wild animals under such conditions and believe that they are being educated? To learn about wild animals, one must observe them in the wild where they live.

4 Zoos also claim that they are conserving **endangered species** in the hope of returning them to the wild in the future. Out of about 10,000 zoos that exist around the world, only a small number register their animals with an international species **database**, and only a small percent of those zoos actually work with endangered species.

5 Zoos have projects where they breed animals in zoos for the purpose of conservation. However, most animals do not need help in breeding; they have been doing it for a long time without any help. Animals have been endangered because humans have destroyed their natural surroundings. One example was the golden lion tamarin[6], a species of monkey that had almost become **extinct** because humans destroyed its natural habitat, and too many were captured for pets and zoos. Over 100 tamarins were bred in zoos, and when they were released into the wild, less than half survived. Some were unable to live life in the wild—they were not able to climb trees, or when they did, they fell off; some did not even move; some were not used to a natural diet. It is a risky business to reintroduce zoo-bred animals to the wild, because if they have lost their **instinct** for survival and cannot **adapt** quickly enough, they will die.

6 In conclusion, it seems that zoos are trying to fulfill their goals to educate and conserve but in the process are harming the animals themselves. What is the solution, then? One solution is to protect the natural homes or habitats of animals. Another possibility is to have habitat preserves where wild animals live with the least possible human interference. If the money and expertise that zoos are using today were redirected to habitat preservation and management, we would not have the problems of having to conserve species whose natural homes have disappeared. Without a doubt, there has to be an international effort to control pollution of habitats and the illegal capturing of endangered species.

---

4 zoochosis 动物精神病
5 Bristol 布里斯托尔，英国西部的港口
6 tamarin 绢毛猴，南美洲产

Vocabulary

Vocabulary in Context

A Complete these sentences with the words or phrases in the box.

adapt	conserve	dignity	extinct	pacing up and down
confined	database	endangered species	instinct	was founded

1. When you are walking back and forth as if worried, you are _____.

2. When animals or humans do things naturally, without learning, they do it by _____.

3. When there are so few examples of a kind of animal or plant that it might die out completely, it is a(n) _____.

4. An animal or plant that no longer exists is _____.

5. A person or animal that has _____ has self-respect and a nobleness of character.

6. The year an organization such as the Zoological Society of London was started or established is the date it _____.

7. To save is to _____.

8. Some zoos have a(n) _____ with lists of endangered animals.

9. Something or someone in a cage or prison is _____.

10. To change so as to be able to live or work in new conditions is to _____.

B Answer these questions with complete sentences.

1. What can your **instinct** tell you sometimes?

2. When do people usually **pace up and down**?

3. What is something that is hard to **adapt** to when you change countries or schools?

4. What is something you can do to **conserve** electricity?

5. What is an animal that is **extinct** today?

Unit 7 Environment 143

C Now write your own sentences. Use the following words in the sentences: ***endangered species***, ***confined***, ***database***, ***dignity***, and ***was founded***.

_____
_____
_____
_____
_____

Vocabulary Building

Complete these sentences with the correct form of the **bold** words. You may use your dictionary.

1. **conserve**
   a. We have had little rain this year and have to _____ water.
   b. They are raising money for elephant _____.

2. **extinct**
   a. Animals like the Sumatran tiger are on their way to _____.
   b. Some ancient civilizations are now _____.

3. **adapt**
   a. Manufacturers _____ this camera for underwater use.
   b. The _____ of the bear to live on the snow and ice as a "polar bear" is quite remarkable.

Reading Comprehension

A Circle the letter of the best answer.

1. Which of the following best expresses the main idea of this passage?
   a. The function of zoos.
   b. The cruelty of shutting animals in zoos.
   c. The importance of natural habitats.
   d. The best way to protect animals.

2. In the author's opinion, animals in zoos _____.
   a. will be stronger and healthier
   b. behave just the same as those outside zoos
   c. lose their dignity
   d. will learn new abilities

3. In which century were the first zoos built?

   a. 17th.

   b. 18th.

   c. 19th.

   d. 20th.

4. On the whole, people's opinion of the zoo is _____.

   a. positive

   b. negative

   c. indifferent

   d. objective

5. Which of the following is true?

   a. In the future there will be more endangered species.

   b. Animals like zoos.

   c. People put animals in zoos to protect them.

   d. With human help, animals breed well.

B Each of the following statements contains information given in the passage. Identify the paragraph from which the information is derived.

1. People pay no attention to animals dignity.   Paragraph _____
2. Some animals have lost their instinct.   Paragraph _____
3. Animals cannot breed well in zoos.   Paragraph _____
4. It is wrong to think that people go to the zoo for education.   Paragraph _____
5. Some animals are endangered.   Paragraph _____

Critical Thinking

Discuss these questions with your classmates.

1. Are zoos necessary? What additional arguments can you find in favor of zoos?

2. Do you think zoos are educational? Why or why not?

3. If we keep zoos, how do you think animals should be kept in them?

4. What do you think are the greatest dangers to the survival of wild animals on our planet today?

5. What can be done to protect endangered wild animals? Do you think it's important to preserve them in the modern world? Why or why not?

Reading 2

Pre-Reading

Preparing for the Reading Topic

A Discuss these questions with your classmates.

1. What do you look for when you are buying fruits or vegetables?
2. Why are chemicals used to grow fruits and vegetables?
3. Would you buy fruits and vegetables grown with chemicals?

B Match the words with their meanings, and tell how you think each word might be connected to the topic of genetically modified food. Then after you have read "Crops, Codes, and Controversy", check your answers.

_____ 1. pesticide   a. lack of water
_____ 2. herbicide   b. lack of food
_____ 3. fertilizer   c. substance that kills plants
_____ 4. drought   d. substance that kills insects
_____ 5. hunger   e. substance that makes plants grow better

Key Vocabulary

As you read "Crops, Codes, and Controversy", pay attention to the following words and phrases and see if you can work out their meanings from the context.

determine	developing countries
resistant	scarce
pests	weeds
nutritional value	absorb
exceed	risks

Crops, Codes, and Controversy

A crop duster sprays pesticide over fields in San Joaquin Valley, California.

1   Over the past 20 years, scientists have been using technology on nature to improve food supplies. They are producing genetically modified (GM) foods by modifying, or changing, the genes of plants and animals. Genes are the codes in the cells of every living thing that determine the way things look and grow. In humans, genes **determine** characteristics such as the color of our eyes and how tall we are. By changing the genes of plants, scientists can cause crops to produce more, become **resistant** to **pests** and disease, and have more **nutritional value**. Genetically modified plants can have great benefits by increasing food supplies, protecting the environment, and even improving nutrition.

2   How will we feed a growing population? The world's population is expected to

A scientist in Laguna, Philippines, examines experimental golden rice.

exceed eight billion by 2025. Much of this increase will occur in the cities of **developing countries**. Unfortunately, food production, instead of increasing, has decreased over the last 10 years. As it is, some 40,000 people die from hunger-related causes every day. The only way to increase food production seems to be through technology, since land and water are getting **scarce**. In Africa, millions of people don't have enough food to eat and are dying because drought has destroyed their food supply. If GM food crops could be developed that could resist droughts or grow in poor, dry, or salty soils, this would help poorer countries.

3   GM crops can protect the environment because they are kinder to nature. Many farmers today depend on chemicals such as pesticides, herbicides, and fertilizers to make their crops grow. Through gene biology, the genes of plants can be modified so that they will be disease-resistant and pest-resistant and still produce the same amount. The most common GM crops grown at the moment are those that resist herbicides. The second most common are those crops that kill pests. Some crops have been grown with both these genes. If a crop can resist herbicides, the farmer can spray a field with herbicides without harming the crop. All the **weeds** and other plants die, but the crop does not. By decreasing the number of weeds, the farmer increases the amount of crop grown. A good example of such a crop is GM cotton, which is often grown in the United States for cottonseed oil. If a crop can kill pests, the farmer does not have to spray so often to kill pests. An example of a pest-resistant crop is maize, which is similar to corn. There is a bacterium in the soil which produces a poison that kills insects, but it is harmless to people. Putting this bacterium gene into maize plants makes them produce their own poison, which kills the pests that eat them. This is better for the environment because it reduces the need to spray fields with pesticides and fertilizers.

4   Genetically modified crops may make food more nutritious by adding genes to produce more vitamins that the body needs for health and growth. For example, a kind of rice called golden rice has been genetically modified to contain vitamin A. Regular rice does not have vitamin A, and some people who live mostly on rice are missing this important vitamin. This new golden rice can make a big difference to those people. Modifying potatoes to contain less starch would make French fries healthier because they would not **absorb** so much fat in the cooking. GM vegetables of the future may be produced with added nutrients to help fight heart disease and cancer.

5   The United States grows 75 percent of the world's GM crops. More than 80 percent of the corn, 85 percent of the cotton, and 90 percent of the soybeans grown in the United States in 2014 were genetically modified. The ingredients from these crops—especially

soy, which is used in many products—show up in a lot of the food we eat, from pizza, cookies, pasta, ice cream, and potato chips, to soup. Are there **risks** to our health and environment from GM foods? Only time and more research will tell.

Vocabulary

A What are the meanings of the **bold** words? Circle the letter of the best answer.

1. Crops are becoming **resistant** to disease.
    a. unaffected by
    b. responsive to
    c. likely to
    d. used to

2. **Pests** damage plants we grow for food.
    a. insects that live on flowers
    b. small animals or insects that destroy crops
    c. animals you buy to keep at home
    d. small animals that live in fields

3. GM crops can have more **nutritional value**.
    a. good characteristics
    b. scientific benefits
    c. chemical meaning
    d. importance to the body as food

4. By 2025, the number of people in the world is going to **exceed** eight billion.
    a. go over
    b. become
    c. get near
    d. be equal to

5. The population is expected to increase in **developing countries**.
    a. countries that are growing in industry
    b. poor countries that are not yet industrialized
    c. countries that are rich and industrialized
    d. countries that are getting bigger in size

6. As time goes by, land and water is becoming **scarce**.
    a. hard to find
    b. rich in quality
    c. poor in quality
    d. increased

7. In humans, genes **determine** our characteristics.
    a. mix up
    b. decide
    c. confuse
    d. collect

8. The crops don't die, but the **weeds** die.
    a. plants that are not healthy
    b. wild plants that grow where you don't want them to grow
    c. animals that eat the plants
    d. insects that live on plants

9. GM potatoes do not **absorb** much oil.
    a. pick out
    b. take in
    c. make up
    d. break up

10. At this time, we do not know the **risks** of GM foods.

    a. dangers
    b. warnings
    c. benefits
    d. advantages

B Answer these questions with complete sentences.

1. What is something that can **absorb** water?
   _____
   _____

2. What is in shortage in most **developing countries**?
   _____
   _____

3. What is a common household **pest**?
   _____
   _____

4. What is something you wear that is **resistant to** water?
   _____
   _____

5. What food do you think has good **nutritional value**?
   _____
   _____

C Now write your own sentences. Use the following words in the sentences: **exceed**, **determine**, **weeds**, **scarce**, and **risks**.

_____
_____
_____
_____
_____

Reading Comprehension

A Circle the letter of the best answer.

1. GM foods will benefit food supplies _____.

    a. around the world
    b. in Africa only
    c. in developing countries only
    d. for animals only

2. According to the reading, GM crops _____.

    a. are better for nature
    b. have herbicides
    c. give problems to farmers
    d. kill other plants

3. GM crops _____.

   a. can absorb more water
   b. are better for cooking
   c. all have vitamin A
   d. can be more nutritious

4. What is the only way to increase food production?

   a. Through better fertilizer.
   b. Through technology.
   c. Through more work force.
   d. Through advanced industrialization.

5. By _____, the farmer increases the amount of crop grown.

   a. increasing the number of weeds
   b. increasing the number of working hours
   c. decreasing the number of weeds
   d. decreasing the number of working hours

B Each of the following statements contains information given in the passage. Identify the paragraph from which the information is derived.

1. Food production has declined rather than increase over the last decade.   Paragraph _____

2. Scientists have been improving food supplies by means of technology in the last twenty years.   Paragraph _____

3. GM crops can be environment-friendly by reducing the amount of some chemicals.   Paragraph _____

4. GM vegetables, with some nutrients added, will treat intractable diseases in the future.   Paragraph _____

Critical Thinking

Discuss these questions with your classmates.

1. What are some possible disadvantages of GM foods?

2. Many foods in supermarkets, such as tomatoes and potatoes in the United States, are genetically modified. Would you buy GM foods? Why or why not?

3. Some animals used for food, such as salmon and pigs, can be genetically modified to grow more quickly. Do you think this is a good idea? Why or why not?

4. Do you think what are the reasons why food production has decreased over the last decade? How can these problems be overcome?

5. What are some of the greatest threats to human survival on our planet today? Do you think we will be able to solve these problems? Why or why not?

Writing

Writing Skills

> **Relevant Support**
>
> It is important for your argument to have *relevant support*. In other words, your support should be directly connected to the argument.
>
> - After giving reasons with relevant and specific details to support your argument, you can conclude with one of the following:
>
>   As a result,...   Finally,...   For these reasons,...   In conclusion,...   Thus,...

Exercise 1

Decide if the following statements are **R** (*Relevant*) or **NR** (*Not Relevant*) to the argument below.

Argument: Ecotourism is the new force in the preservation of animals.

_____ 1. It works in cooperation with the people of the surrounding area, and alternative jobs are given to hunters.

_____ 2. The best guides are often ex-hunters who discourage others from illegal hunting.

_____ 3. People will be able to watch wildlife in their natural habitats.

_____ 4. Nature-based tourism has been practiced for decades in national parks and other protected areas without any problems.

_____ 5. High levels of ecotourism will not be compatible with the environment.

_____ 6. For reasons of age, health, or money, many people will not be able to go on these trips.

Exercise 2

Read the following essay written by a student. Then answer the questions at the end of the essay.

> **Argument for Zoos**
>
> In the past, zoos were places where we saw single animals in small, empty cages. Today, zoos are changing in design; animals have more space, and some live in groups. Many zoos try to put animals in an environment that is similar to where they live in the wild. Some people who believe in animal rights argue against having zoos, because they think it is wrong to put animals in cages. I support the idea of having zoos, because they allow us to see wild animals that we cannot see otherwise, and they help endangered species from becoming extinct.

Giant panda cub born in San Diego Zoo in 2005

   The first reason for having zoos is that they allow people to see wild animals that they could not see otherwise. Zoos are the only places for most people who live in cities to see wild animals. Seeing wild animals on nature documentary programs or in books is not the same thing as seeing animals in real life. Zoos educate people about wild animals and teach them to understand and care about them. That is why there are school trips to the zoo, where the zookeepers tell students about the animals.

   Secondly, many endangered species would become extinct if we did not have zoos. Zoos have saved numerous species from dying out or have helped animals get healthier and returned them back to the wild. For example, the San Diego Zoo in California has special programs to save the giant pandas and white rhinoceroses. There is also a great deal of research that goes on in many zoos to study animal behavior.

   In conclusion, zoos have a valuable role to play: they educate the public and help preserve certain species. It is important for animals to be treated well and kept in an environment that is as natural as possible. Many zoos today are responding to their critics and changing the way they keep animals so that they can continue their role without harming animals.

1. What is the thesis statement? Circle it.
2. What is the topic sentence in each of the body paragraphs? Underline them.
3. Which supporting sentences in the two body paragraphs are facts? Write **F** over them.
4. Which supporting sentences in the two body paragraphs are opinions? Write **O** over them.

Using Factual Details to Support Your Opinion

It is important to support your opinions with *factual details*. The more concrete your facts are, the more convincing your argument will be.

- When using facts, refer to a reliable authority and identify it by name. In the following examples, the facts are given by the Australia New Zealand Food Authority and the UN's Food and Agriculture Organization. These are the authorities.

    EXAMPLES: *Fact without support:* In some countries, the GM foods are labeled.

    Concrete supporting detail: According to the Australia New Zealand Food Authority, after December 7, 2001, any GM food, either whole or an ingredient in processed food, must be labeled.

    Fact without support: Many people around the world are hungry.

    Concrete supporting detail: According to the UN's Food and Agriculture Organization (FAO; 1996), one in seven of the world's population is chronically malnourished.

- Vague references to authority are not acceptable in an argument. Do not use such phrases as *They say...* or *People say...* or *Authorities agree...* Do not use a relative or a friend as an authority.

- Remember to introduce your examples with *for example*, *for instance*, or *e.g.* (from Latin *exempli gratia*, meaning "for example").

Exercise 3

Check (✓) the statements that use reliable sources.

_____ 1. Certain foods can be genetically modified to be better.

_____ 2. According to the journal *Nature* (Vol. 419, 2002), a GM onion that will not make our eyes water can be produced.

_____ 3. About 60 to 70 percent of packaged foods in the United States contain GM ingredients, said Hansen, a research associate with the Consumer Policy Institute in New York (2002).

_____ 4. Europeans say that Americans eat a lot of GM foods.

_____ 5. They say that GM foods may one day harm the environment.

Exercise 4

Match the following statements with the factual details below that support them.

_____ 1. Research to date seems to indicate that genetically modified foods are safe to eat.

_____ 2. People are questioning the dangers that GM crops may pose to our wildlife.

_____ 3. Europeans are generally against GM crops, and Americans also are expressing concern.

_____ 4. All countries need to reduce the impact of agriculture on our planet's environment.

_____ 5. Genetically modified foods have become an essential part of U.S. agriculture.

_____ 6. GM crops are reducing some of our worries about global food production in the future.

_____ 7. It is difficult to reassure people that genetically modified food is safe.

a. According to Dr. Marc Van Montagu, Chairman of the Ghent University Institute of Plant Biotechnology, it is much easier to prove to people that a danger exists than it is to show that no danger exists.

b. The World Health Organization, for example, is concerned that the GMO may escape and introduce the engineered genes into wild plant populations in the environment.

c. For example, the Pew Initiative on Food and Biotechnology has found that the majority of corn, soy, and cotton grown by U.S. farmers today are from genetically engineered seeds.

d. According to the World Resources Institute, there will be a need to feed more than 9 billion people by 2050.

e. According to the World Health Organization, foods that are on the international market have passed many risk assessment tests and are unlikely to be a danger to human health.

f. For instance, a recent CBS/New York Times poll states that 53 percent of Americans say they won't buy food that has been genetically modified.

g. According to the World Resources Institute, modern agriculture produces gases that contribute to global warming and is the main cause of tropical deforestation.

Writing Practice

Write an Essay

Choose one of the following topics to write an argument essay.

1. GM plants or animals
2. Organic farming
3. Using pesticides or fertilizers

Pre-Write

A Work with a partner and brainstorm examples for your topic.

B Make a list of your examples, and work on a thesis statement for your essay.

Outline

Fill in the outline below. Write your thesis statement for the topic of your essay, and pick the two best examples from Exercise B in Pre-Write for the topics of your body paragraphs. Finally, write your conclusion.

Essay Outline

Introduction
Thesis statement: _____
_____

Body Paragraph 1
Topic sentence: _____
_____

    Supporting detail 1: _____
    Supporting detail 2: _____

Body Paragraph 2
Topic sentence: _____
_____

    Supporting detail 1: _____
    Supporting detail 2: _____

Conclusion
Restatement of thesis: _____
_____

Final comment: _____

Write and Revise Your Essay

Translation

A Translate the following passage into English.

景泰蓝（Cloisonné）是一种古老的装饰金属物品的工艺。采用这项工艺生产出的物品也可以称为景泰蓝。这种工艺的制作流程是这样的：首先要通过焊接（solder）或粘贴工艺用银线或金线给金属物件勾边，以将其分隔为几个小块。这些金银线在成品上依然能看到，它们将瓷釉或镶嵌物（enamel or inlays）的不同部分分隔开来，通常这些瓷釉或镶嵌物会有多种颜色。这项工艺至今在中国仍然很常见。

B Translate the following passage into Chinese.

The famous Italian traveler Marco Polo was so impressed by the beauty of Hangzhou that he described it as "the most fascinating city in the world where one feels that one is in paradise". In China, there is a century-old popular saying praising the city, "In the heaven there is Paradise; on the earth there are Suzhou and Hangzhou." Hangzhou's fame lies mainly in its picturesque West Lake. As it is beautiful all the year round, the West Lake was compared by Su Dongpo, a celebrated poet of the Song Dynasty, to a beauty "who is always charming in either light or heavy makeup". In Hangzhou, you will not only find the lake a perfect delight to the eye but also find it a joy to stroll along the busy streets, taste famous Hangzhou dishes and buy some special local products.

Weaving It Together

Unit Project

In this part, you are required to do some research among your classmates, friends or relatives. Collect information about their attitudes towards the environment. Then give a presentation to your classmates. The following questions can be used as references.

1. How to protect our environment?
2. How to develop a low-carbon economy?
3. How to improve the relationship between men and the environment?
4. How to solve global warming?
5. What are advantages and shortcomings of renewable resources?

Searching the Internet

A Search the Internet for information about GM food. Find answers to these questions:

1. What do you think are the possible risks of GM food?
2. What are the benefits of GM food?
3. Did your research change your opinion about GM food? Why or why not?

B Search the Internet for information about one organization that is dedicated to protecting animals and the environment. Share the information with your classmates.

What Do You Think Now?

Refer to Page 139 at the beginning of this unit. Do you know the answers now? Complete the sentence, or circle the best answer.

1. Zoos (do/don't) exist only to entertain people.
2. Some animals (get/do not get) a condition called zoochosis from being in a zoo.
3. The United States (grows/doesn't grow) the most genetically modified crops.
4. Genetically modified crops are more _____.

Broadening Your Horizon

A

What are Genetically Modified GM Foods?

Man has been "genetically modifying" everything from food to dogs for many centuries; but in the past, the only tool has been selective breeding. For example, if you wanted to create a breed of corn with resistance to a certain fungus, you would plant a plot of corn and see how individual plants did with the fungus. Then you would take seeds from the plants that did well, plant them, look at their performance against the fungus… and so on over the years until you had created a strain of corn plant that had very high resistance to the fungus in question.

B

AAAS: Don't Label GM Foods

Slapping labels on genetically modified (GM) foods is a bad idea, according to the American Association for the Advancement of Science (AAAS). The science advocacy organization's executive board approved a statement on October 20th saying that requiring such labels, as a ballot measure in California seeks to do, could "mislead and falsely alarm consumers".

C

General Information About GM Foods

People have been manipulating the genetic make-up of plants and animals for countless generations. This is referred to as traditional cross breeding and involves selecting plants and animals with the most desirable characteristics (e.g. disease resistance, high yield, good meat quality) for breeding the next generation.

Unit 7 Environment

UNIT 8
Readings from Literature

WHAT DO YOU THINK?

Answer these questions with your best guess. Circle *Yes* or *No*.

1. Can a poem have more than one meaning? Yes No
2. Do the words in poems create pictures in our mind? Yes No
3. Do fables teach us lessons? Yes No
4. Do fables only have animals as characters? Yes No

Merton College Library, Oxford, England

Reading 1

Pre-Reading

Preparing for the Reading Topic

A Discuss these questions with your classmates.

1. Do you like to take walks in nature? Why or why not?
2. Do some people know from an early age what road they are going to travel in life? Did you know?
3. What is a simple decision you have made today? What is a more difficult decision you have made recently?

B Match the six expressions about life with their possible meanings below. Then after you have read "The Road Not Taken", review your answers.

_____ 1. Come to a fork in the road

_____ 2. Choose a path

_____ 3. Take the road less traveled

_____ 4. Look down the road

_____ 5. One road leads to another

_____ 6. Look back

a. try to see the future

b. one decision leads to other decisions

c. think about the past

d. make a decision

e. reach a time when a decision has to be made

f. do something different from most people

Key Vocabulary

As you read, "The Road Not Taken", pay attention to the following words and see if you can work out their meanings from the context.

diverged	wear
bent	equally
fair	step
claim	doubted
grassy	sigh

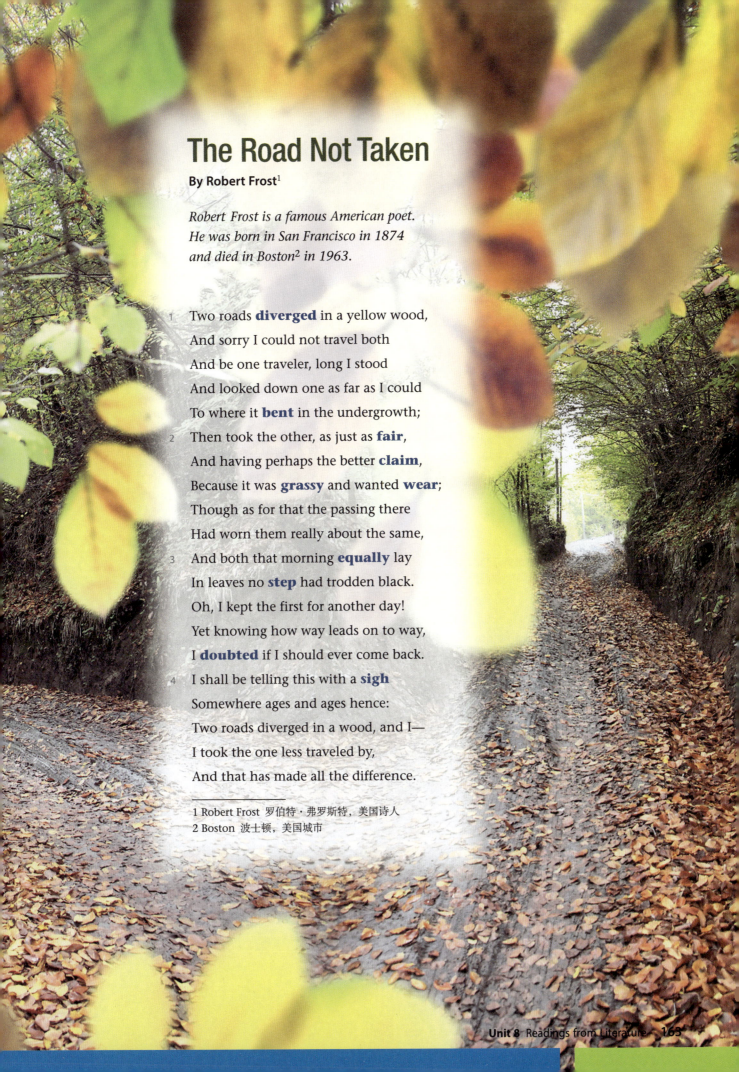

The Road Not Taken

By Robert Frost[1]

Robert Frost is a famous American poet. He was born in San Francisco in 1874 and died in Boston[2] in 1963.

1 Two roads **diverged** in a yellow wood,
And sorry I could not travel both
And be one traveler, long I stood
And looked down one as far as I could
To where it **bent** in the undergrowth;

2 Then took the other, as just as **fair**,
And having perhaps the better **claim**,
Because it was **grassy** and wanted **wear**;
Though as for that the passing there
Had worn them really about the same,

3 And both that morning **equally** lay
In leaves no **step** had trodden black.
Oh, I kept the first for another day!
Yet knowing how way leads on to way,
I **doubted** if I should ever come back.

4 I shall be telling this with a **sigh**
Somewhere ages and ages hence:
Two roads diverged in a wood, and I—
I took the one less traveled by,
And that has made all the difference.

---

1 Robert Frost 罗伯特·弗罗斯特，美国诗人
2 Boston 波士顿，美国城市

Vocabulary

Vocabulary in Context

A Complete these sentences with the words in the box.

| bent | diverged | equally | grassy | step |
| claim | doubted | fair | sigh | wear |

1. A(n) _____ place is covered in green growth low on the ground.
2. If you _____ something, you expected that it was not true or would probably not happen.
3. A(n) _____ is a sound made when a person lets out a deep breath, showing tiredness, sadness, or pleasure.
4. When something _____, it separated and went in different directions.
5. _____ is as much or to the same degree.
6. When something is used over and over, it shows _____.
7. Something _____ is beautiful and attractive.
8. Something is _____ when at a certain point it curved or turned at an angle.
9. To take a(n) _____ is to put one foot down in front of the other.
10. A(n) _____ is a statement of something as fact or truth.

B Answer these questions with complete sentences.

1. Where is a **grassy** place you like to visit?
   _____
   _____

2. In what way can clothes show **wear**?
   _____
   _____

3. In what situation would you **sigh**?
   _____
   _____

4. What are two activities that you like to do **equally**?
   _____
   _____

5. When have you **doubted** your ability to do something?
   _____
   _____

C Now write your own sentences. Use the following words in the sentences: **step**, **claim**, **bent**, **fair**, and ***diverged***.

_____
_____
_____
_____
_____

Vocabulary Building

Complete these sentences with the correct form of the **bold** words. You may use your dictionary.

1. **diverged**
   a. My friend and I have _____ views on what movie we want to see.
   b. There is a small island where the river _____.

2. **doubt**
   a. It's _____ that we'll buy a new car this year.
   b. There's no _____ that tomorrow will be as hot as it is today.

3. **equally**
   a. The patients all received an _____ amount of care.
   b. The cake was divided _____ among the children.

Reading Comprehension

A Circle the letter of the best answer.

1. Which of the following best expresses the meaning of lines 2 and 3 in the first stanza?
   a. The traveler is eager to travel the roads.
   b. The traveler knows exactly which way he wants to go.
   c. The traveler knows he has to choose one road.
   d. The traveler wishes he were with another traveler.

2. Lines 4 and 5 in the first stanza tell us that the traveler _____.
   a. is trying to see where the road goes
   b. knows where each road goes
   c. can see that the road ends a little way ahead
   d. can't see the road at all

3. In the second stanza, lines 4 and 5 show that the traveler _____.
   a. decides one road has been traveled more
   b. doesn't know which road has had more travelers
   c. questions whether either road has been traveled
   d. decides the roads have been equally traveled

4. The two lines in the third stanza "Yet knowing how way leads on to way, I doubted if I should ever come back." mean the traveler _____.

   a. thinks he might regret his decision

   b. knows his decision is final

   c. thinks he might change his mind someday

   d. doesn't know if he's making the right decision

5. What does the writer want to tell us in the last stanza?

   a. He made the wrong decision.

   b. The decision he made was important for his life.

   c. He made the right decision.

   d. The decision he made didn't change his life much.

B Each statement below contains information given in the passage. Identify the paragraph from which the information is derived.

1. The regret hangs over the traveler like a heavy cloud about to burst. He realizes that he will have regrets about having never gone back and traveling down the roads he did not take.   Stanza _____

2. As much the traveler may strain his eyes to see as far the road stretches, eventually it surpasses his vision and he can never see where it is going to lead.   Stanza _____

3. Once you have performed an act or spoken a word that crystallizes who you are, there is no turning back and it cannot be undone.   Stanza _____

4. The fact that the traveler took this path over the more popular, secure one indicates the type of personality he has, one that does not want to necessarily follow the crowd but do more of what has never been done, what is new and different.   Stanza _____

5. It is always difficult to make a decision because it is impossible not to wonder about the opportunity lost.   Stanza _____

Critical Thinking

Discuss these questions with your classmates.

1. What do you think is the symbolic meaning of two roads in the poem? Why?

2. In what way are we all "travelers on the road of life"? Illustrate it with some facts and examples.

3. Have you ever regretted a decision that you made? Why or why not? Why is it difficult to go back after we have made certain choices in life?

4. The traveler in the poem says that both roads are about the same. But he says that later in life he will tell people that he took "the one less traveled by". Why do you think the traveler is going to tell a different story from what really happened?

5. What does it mean to "take the easy way out"? Do you think most people try to take that way? Why or why not? In your life, do you want to take the easy way out or the road less traveled? Explain why.

Reading ▪2

Pre-Reading

Preparing for the Reading Topic

A Discuss these questions with your classmates.

1. Why is working hard important in life? What are some of the results of hard work?
2. Is it possible to make a fortune by starting with nothing at all? Why or why not?
3. In what ways can people show they are grateful for someone's help?

B Work with a partner. Talk about the ways that each of the following qualities can help someone succeed in business.

- intelligence
- desire to work hard
- gratitude
- creativity
- boldness

Key Vocabulary

As you read "The Story of the Mouse Merchant", pay attention to the following words and see if you can work out their meanings from the context.

capital	receipt
fortune	a burst of laughter
loans	collected
scolding	shrewd
interest	solid

Statue of a golden mouse from a temple in Maharashtra, India

Unit 8 Readings from Literature 167

The Story of the Mouse Merchant

From An Argosy of Fables[1], *selected and edited by Frederic Taber Cooper*[2] *(1921).*

1 Many men have started with very little **capital** and have ended with great wealth. But I built up my large **fortune** by starting with nothing at all. Listen, and you shall hear how I did it.

2 My father died before I was born; and my mother's wicked relatives took everything she had. To save her life, my mother got away from her relatives and stayed at the home of one of my father's friends. I was born there and later became my mother's protector. Meanwhile, she supported us by the little she earned through her hard work. And even though we were so poor, she found a teacher who agreed to teach me the basics of reading, writing, and arithmetic.

3 Then one day my mother said to me, "Son, your father used to be a merchant, and now it's time for you to become a merchant, too. The richest merchant now living in our city is the moneychanger, Visakhila, and I've heard that he makes **loans** to the poor sons of good families to help them start their own business. Go to him and ask him for a loan."

4 I went to the moneychanger and found him angrily **scolding** another merchant's son, to whom he had loaned money. "See that mouse on the ground?" he asked. "A clever man could start with even such poor capital as a mouse and make a fortune. But, however much money I loan you, I can just get back the **interest** on it, and I doubt if I will ever get back any of the money I gave you."

5 Without thinking I turned to Visakhila and said, "I will accept the dead mouse as capital to start my own business!"

6 With these words, I picked up the mouse, wrote a **receipt**, and went on my way, leaving the moneychanger in **a burst of laughter**.

---

1 *An Argosy of Fables* 《寓言之船》
2 Frederic Taber Cooper 弗雷德里克·泰伯·库珀，美国作家

7   I sold the mouse as cat's meat to another merchant, for two handfuls of peas. I ground the peas and along with a pitcher³ of water, I went out of the city and sat under the shade of a big tree. Many tired wood-cutters passed by, carrying their wood to market. To each one, I politely offered a drink of cool water and a serving of peas. Every wood-cutter was thankful and gave me a couple of sticks of wood in payment. At the end of the day, I took these sticks and sold them in the market. Then with a part of the money I received from the sale of the wood, I bought a new supply of peas; and so on the second day, I obtained more sticks from the wood-cutters.

Within a few days I had **collected** quite a small amount of capital and was able to buy all the wood that the wood-cutters could cut in three days. Soon, because of heavy rains, wood was scarce in the market, and I was able to sell all that I had bought for several hundred panas⁴. With this money I started a shop, and as I am a **shrewd** businessman I soon became wealthy.

8   Then I went to a goldsmith and had him make me a mouse of **solid** gold. I presented this mouse to Visakhila as payment of the loan. Soon after, he allowed me to marry his daughter. Because of this story I am known to the world as Mushika, the Mouse. So this is how I made a fortune without any capital.

---

3 pitcher 带柄的陶罐
4 panas 一种古印度金币

Vocabulary

A What are the meanings of the **bold** words? Circle the letter of the best answer.

1. Some companies begin with very little **capital** and yet become very successful.
   a. money earned by selling things
   b. money borrowed for a long period of time
   c. money found where there was none before
   d. money used to start a business

2. Some people can make a **fortune** by owning their own business.
   a. a certain amount of good luck
   b. a small profit or gain
   c. a big loss
   d. a large amount of money

3. Many people take out **loans** to start a business.
   a. money given to use for a certain length of time
   b. money given as a gift to someone
   c. money saved over a long period of time
   d. money provided to those who help others

4. The moneychanger was **scolding** a merchant's son.
   a. speaking in an angry, complaining way
   b. hurting in a physical way
   c. expressing one's happiness about
   d. talking in a quiet way about

5. The moneychanger charged **interest** on his loans.
   a. an amount reduced from one's bill
   b. money paid for the use of money
   c. extra money given to the borrower
   d. money given away for free

6. The young man gave a **receipt** for the mouse.
   a. a bill for the cost of something bought
   b. a promise to pay back a loan
   c. a statement listing money or goods received
   d. a request for goods or services

7. The moneychanger gave a **burst of laughter**.
   a. a quiet expression of pleasure
   b. a loud and sudden expression of amusement
   c. a long muttering under one's breath
   d. an unexpected voice showing anger

8. The young man **collected** money from the sale of his wood.
   a. made
   b. saved
   c. gathered together
   d. gave away

9. The poor boy became a **shrewd** businessman.
   a. clever
   b. strange
   c. trusting
   d. successful

10. He had a mouse made of **solid** gold.
    a. some part of
    b. a mixture of
    c. completely of
    d. nothing inside of

B Answer these questions with complete sentences.

1. When do you ask for a **receipt**?

   _____

2. What might cause you to give a **burst of laughter**?

   _____

3. What is something you **collected** as a child?

   _____

4. What is something people commonly take out **loans** for?

   _____

5. By doing what might a child receive a **scolding**?

   _____

C Now write your own sentences. Use the following words in the sentences: **shrewd**, **fortune**, **interest**, **solid**, and **capital**.

_____

_____

_____

_____

Reading Comprehension

A Circle the letter of the best answer.

1. Where did the boy and his mother live?
    a. They lived in the home of one of his father's relatives.
    b. They lived in the home of one of his mother's relatives.
    c. They lived in the home of one of his father's friends.
    d. They lived in the home of one of his mother's friends.

2. Why did the mother send her son to Visakhila?
    a. Because she wanted her son to become a merchant.
    b. Because she wanted her son to ask Visakhila for a loan.
    c. Because she wanted her son to learn how to make money.
    d. Because she wanted her son to borrow some money from Visakhila.

3. What did Visakhila think he would get from another merchant's son?
    a. He thought he would only get back the interest on the loan he gave to him.
    b. He thought he would only get the loan from him.
    c. He thought he would get such poor capital as a mouse from him.
    d. He thought he would get nothing but a little capital from him.

4. What did the young man do with the dead mouse?

   a. He sold it to the woodcutters for two handfuls of peas.

   b. He offered it to the woodcutters for some sticks.

   c. He sold it in the market and got some sticks with the money.

   d. He sold it to another merchant for two handfuls of peas.

5. What was the young man able to do with the money he made from selling all his wood?

   a. He was able to buy more wood sticks.

   b. He was able to start a shop.

   c. He was able to buy more peas.

   d. He was able to make a mouse of solid gold.

B An introductory sentence for a brief summary of Reading 2 is provided below. Complete the summary with a few more sentences.

This story tells us how a merchant built up his fortune by starting his business with nothing.

_____
_____
_____
_____
_____
_____
_____
_____

Critical Thinking

Discuss these questions with your classmates.

1. Fables have been written for thousands of years. What purpose do they serve? Why are they so popular?

2. In the fable, the mother says the son should be a merchant like his father. Some parents want their sons to work in the same profession. Should children be forced to have the careers their parents want for them? Why or why not?

3. What does success mean to you?

4. Do you think that success and financial wealth bring happiness? Why or why not?

5. Do you think that success always comes from hard work? Why or why not? Do most people need help to become successful? Explain why.

Writing

Writing Skills

Imagery

To make a poem more interesting and meaningful, writers use words to create a picture of something in our mind, or *imagery*. These images make ideas seem real to us. They also give added meaning to a poem. To make an image or picture, writers may use colorful words and expressions, or *poetic language*. They may also compare two different things in a descriptive way by using a *metaphor*.

- To create an image, writers use **poetic language** to show sound, color, feeling, taste, smell, and touch.

    EXAMPLES: Two roads diverged in a *yellow* wood.
    I shall be telling this with a *sigh*.

- A **metaphor** compares one thing with another.

    EXAMPLES: *Two roads diverged*
    The two roads going different ways is compared to a choice someone must make.

    Looked down the road
    Looking down the road is compared to trying to see the future.

Exercise 1

Write a descriptive sentence about the following topics. Use words of sound, taste, color, smell, or touch to create vivid images.

1. A seashore

2. A meal

3. An ancient city

4. A morning walk

5. A family event

Exercise 2

Write a sentence about the following topics by using metaphors.

1. A beautiful singing voice

2. A difficult task

3. A calm lake

4. Time

5. Feeling hurt or sad

Writing an Analysis of a Poem

Analyzing a poem helps you to understand it and enjoy it more. To write an analysis of a poem, first you need to understand the basic details of what the poem is about, in other words, the *literal meaning* of the poem. You should reread the poem many times to make sure you can follow the poet's ideas and images.

- When you write about the literal meaning, you may use sentence starters such as the following:

    The poem is about...
    The poet is...
    The setting is...
    The poet sees...

    The poet decides...
    The poet thinks...
    The poet imagines...

The second step to write an analysis of a poem is to read the poem again for the *deeper meaning*. Look at words, lines, phrases, and the use of images to shape your ideas. When you write about the deeper meaning of a poem, quote words, lines, and phrases to show how the writer uses images and metaphors to convey meaning. Pay special attention to the opening and closing lines of the poem.

- When you write about the deeper meaning, you can use sentence starters such as the following:

    The meaning of the poem is...
    The first description of the setting is...
    The first metaphor is...
    The next four lines provide an image of...

    Lines 6–10 describe...
    Line 13 tells us...
    Lines 16 and 17 provide an image of...
    The final metaphor is...

Exercise 3

Look back at your answers to the questions under *Reading Comprehension* on Pages 165–166. Use your answers to write one or two paragraphs explaining the literal and deeper meaning of the poem.

Personal Narrative

The fable of the mouse merchant is written in the style of a personal narrative. A *personal narrative* tells a story in chronological order about experiences or events that have happened or are happening in the writer's life. The writer uses details and personal observations and feelings to make the story come to life and to offer clues about the purpose of the story. The writer may want to inspire, entertain, or give a moral lesson as in a fable.

- **A personal narrative provides details about people, places, and events.** These details convey to the reader why the writer is telling the story. In the excerpt from the story below, the writer emphasizes how hard the mouse merchant worked, doing the same thing over and over to get a little more money each day. This provides a clue to the writer's purpose for telling this story: to show how hard work leads to success.

    EXAMPLE: At the end of the day, I took these sticks and sold them in the market. Then with a part of the money I received from the sale of the wood, I bought a new supply of peas; and so on the second day, I obtained more sticks from the wood-cutters.

- **It is important to use descriptive language in personal narratives.** This allows the reader to have vivid images of what is happening. Nouns, adjectives, and strong action verbs give life to a story by creating clear and real pictures in the reader's mind. It is important to use language that *shows* rather than *tells*.

    EXAMPLE: ***Tell:*** The moneychanger was upset with another merchant's son.
    Show: I went to the moneychanger and found him angrily scolding another merchant's son, to whom he had loaned money. "See that mouse on the ground," he asked …

    Tell: It was a beautiful day.
    Show: The sun was shining brightly, the sky was a deep blue, and the apple blossoms trembled in a light breeze.

    Tell: I had an interesting and exciting time at the science museum today.
    Show: At the science museum today, I saw the animated and life-like dinosaur exhibit and watched a 3-D movie about space travel that made us feel as if we were in the rocket ship ourselves.

Exercise 4

Imagine you are the narrator for each of the following stories. Write three details that would make the story come to life. Then state what purpose each story might have, using the words *inspire*, *entertain*, or *give a moral lesson*.

1. You are an athlete who has overcome difficulties to succeed.

    Details: _____

    _____

    Purpose: _____

2. You are working with a team of people to build a new home for your neighbors.

    Details: _____

    _____

    Purpose: _____

3. A series of disastrous but funny events that have happened to you during a trip.

   Details: _____

   _____

   Purpose: _____

Exercise 5

Use descriptive language, such as nouns, adjectives, and strong action verbs, to rewrite the following descriptions. Create vivid images that *show* rather than *tell*.

1. It's a miserable day outside.

   _____

2. I had a wonderful time in the city today.

   _____

3. Our band had a terrible experience on stage last night.

   _____

4. I had a great time at my cousin's wedding.

   _____

Writing Practice

Write a Personal Narrative

Think of an experience that means a lot to you or that has had a big effect on your life. Think about why you want to tell the story and what details will help explain your purpose.

Pre-Write

A Before you start writing, make notes about each of the following questions.

1. What is the event or experience I want to tell a story about?
2. What is the time order in which the events happened?
3. What details and personal observations do I want to include about my experience?
4. What personal feelings do I want to share about my experience?

B Think about the details that you have decided to include in your personal narrative. Make notes about each of the following questions to help bring your story to life.

1. How can I *show* rather than *tell* about this event or experience?
2. How can I use one or more of the five senses in my descriptions to tell the reader how something looks, tastes, smells, sounds, or feels?
3. How can I use nouns and active verbs to create strong, clear images?
4. How can I use personal observations or quoted conversations to make the details lively and interesting?

Write and Revise Your Essay

Translation

A Translate the following passage into English.

盲人坐在楼前的台阶上，脚边放着块牌子，写着："我是盲人，请帮帮我。"

一位有创意头脑的广告员走过，发现盲人的帽子里只有少许硬币。往帽子里放了些硬币后，他拿过牌子，写了些什么，放回原处后离开了。

傍晚时分，广告员又回到盲人那儿，发现帽子里装满了钞票和硬币。盲人也听出了他的脚步声，问广告员是不是换了他的牌子，还说想知道牌子上写了什么。

其实盲人不知道，牌子上写的是："春天来了，但我却看不到它。"

B Translate the following passage into Chinese.

Once upon a time the Sheep complained to the shepherd about how differently he treated them and his Dog. "Your conduct," said they, "is very strange and, we think, very unfair. We provide you with wool and lambs and milk and you give us nothing but grass, and even that we have to find for ourselves, but you get nothing at all from the Dog, and yet you feed him with tidbits from your own table." Their remarks were overheard by the Dog, who spoke up at once and said, "Yes, and quite right, too. Where would you be if it wasn't for me? Thieves would steal you! Wolves would eat you! Indeed, if I didn't keep constant watch over you, you would be too terrified even to graze!" The Sheep were obliged to acknowledge that he spoke the truth, and never again made a grievance of the way they were treated by his master.

Weaving It Together

Unit Project

In this part, you are required to do some research among your classmates, friends or relatives. Collect information about their experience. Then give a presentation to your classmates. The following questions can be used as references.

1. What kind of interesting or important experience have you ever had?
2. Think of a strange or funny experience you had. Why was it strange or funny?
3. Do you think a certain experience can change one's life? Why or why not?
4. Which do you think is more important, book knowledge or practical experience? Why?
5. How do you understand the statement "Experience makes one more resourceful."?

Searching the Internet

A Search the Internet for information about these famous American poets: Maya Angelou, Emily Dickinson, Langston Hughes, and Walt Whitman. Find answers to these questions:

1. When were they born?
2. What are the general topics or themes that they chose for their poems?
3. What is the title of a famous poem by each poet?

B Search the Internet for some interesting fables from around the world. Share the information with your classmates.

What Do You Think Now?

Refer to Page 160 at the beginning of this unit. Do you know the answers now? Circle the best answer.

1. A poem (can/cannot) have more than one meaning.
2. Words in poems (create/do not create) pictures in our mind.
3. Fables (teach/do not teach) us lessons.
4. Fables (only have/don't only have) animals as characters.

Broadening Your Horizon

About the Author Robert Lee Frost

Robert Lee Frost (March 26, 1874–January 29, 1963) was an American poet. His work was initially published in England before it was published in America. He is highly regarded for his realistic depictions of rural life and his command of American colloquial speech.

What Do You Know About Fables?

Fable is a literary genre, a succinct fictional story, in prose or verse, that features animals, legendary creatures, plants, inanimate objects, or forces of nature that are anthropomorphized (given human qualities, such as the ability to speak human language) and that illustrates or leads to a particular moral lesson (a "moral"), which may at the end be added explicitly as a pithy maxim.

About the Author Frederic Taber Cooper

Frederic Taber Cooper (May 27, 1864–May 20, 1937) was an American editor and writer, born in New York City, and educated at Harvard University and Columbia University. He was an associate professor of Latin and Sanskrit at New York University (1895–1902).

GLOSSARY

A

a matter of		关乎……的事情	U6R1
a variety of		各种各样的	U5R2
absorb	v.	吸收；吸引	U7R2
accommodate	v.	容纳；供应	U2R2
add...to...		添加至……	U6R1
almond	n.	杏仁	U3R1
arrogant	a.	傲慢的	U3R1
as well as		也……	U3R1
astrologer	n.	占星家	U1R2
at a fast pace		迅速；快速	U1R1
auction	n.	拍卖	U2R2
awaken	v.	唤起	U1R1

B

bacterium	n.	细菌	U7R2
be attached to sb.		非常喜爱某人	U3R1
be involved in		参加；相关	U3R2
be sensitive to		对……敏感	U1R1
be supposed to		应该；被期望	U1R1
bold	a.	大胆的	U3R1
bring out		产生	U3R2
brush aside		不理；不顾	U2R1
buffalo	n.	野牛	U4R1
build up		逐渐积聚，增多	U8R2
bulge	n.	凸出部分	U3R1
bump	n.	肿起；隆起物	U3R1
bundles of		很多捆	U2R1

C

canvas	n.	帆布	U2R1
carry out		执行；实行	U7R1
centipede	n.	蜈蚣	U2R2
chin	n.	下巴	U3R1
claim	v.	声称，断言	U1R1
cleanse	v.	净化；使……纯净；使……清洁	U5R1

clueless	a.	无线索的	U6R1
code	n.	代码；密码	U6R1
come out of nowhere		突然出现	U4R1
commission	n.	委员会	U6R2
confine	v.	限制；禁闭	U7R1
conserve	v.	保存；保护	U7R1
consolation	n.	安慰	U2R2
controversy	n.	争论；论战	U7R2
conveyor belt		传送带	U5R1
cope with		处理	U3R2
courageous	a.	勇敢的	U4R2
crack	v.	使破裂；破解	U6R1
criticize	v.	批评；评论	U7R1
crocodile	n.	鳄鱼	U4R1
curve	n.	曲线	U3R1

D

daring	a.	大胆的，勇敢的	U4R1
database	n.	数据库；资料库	U7R1
decode	v.	译码，解码	U6R1
dedicate	v.	献身	U4R1
depression	n.	沮丧	U1R1
detect	v.	发现	U3R2
determined	a.	坚决的	U4R1
dignity	n.	尊严；高贵	U7R1
distinct	a.	有区别的	U5R2
diverge	v.	分叉，岔开	U8R1
diversity	n.	多样性	U2R1
dolphin	n.	海豚	U3R2
dream of		梦想	U4R2

E

eliminate	v.	消除；排除	U6R2
emerge	v.	出现	U2R1
emotion	n.	情绪；情感	U1R1
encounter	v.	遭遇；遇到	U2R1

GLOSSARY

endanger	v.	危及；使遭到危险	U7R1
engage	v.	使订婚	U4R2
entertainment	n.	娱乐	U7R1
entry	n.	进入；入口	U2R2
exceed	v.	超过；胜过	U7R2
extinct	a.	灭绝的，绝种的	U7R1
eyebrow	n.	眉毛	U3R1

F

fertilizer	n.	肥料	U7R2
fill out		填写	U2R2
frustrate	v.	挫败	U2R2
fundamental	a.	基本的	U2R2

G

geographic	a.	地理的	U4R1
get away from		离开	U8R2
get stuck		被卡住；被堵	U6R2
globalization	n.	全球化	U5R2
glow	v.	发热	U2R1
go to great lengths		不遗余力	U1R2
goldsmith	n.	金匠	U8R2
grind	v.	把……磨成粉，研磨	U8R2

H

habitat	n.	生长环境；栖息地	U7R1
have a strong effect on		对……有重大影响	U1R1
heal	v.	治愈；痊愈	U1R1
hence	ad.	从此；因此	U8R1
household	a.	家庭的；日常的	U6R2

I

in celebration of		为庆祝……	U2R1
in conclusion		总之；最后	U7R1
in contrast (with/to)		与……相比	U5R1

in spite of		尽管	U1R2
incite	v.	激励	U2R2
incomprehensible	a.	难以理解的	U6R1
indicate	v.	表明	U3R1
inevitably	ad.	不可避免地	U5R2
ingredient	n.	原料	U5R1
initiative	n.	倡议；首创精神	U4R1
inspiration	n.	灵感	U2R2
instinct	n.	本能；直觉	U7R1
intercept	v.	拦截；窃听	U6R1
interference	n.	干扰；冲突	U7R1
invisible	a.	看不见的	U6R1

J

jealous	a.	妒忌的	U1R1
jockey	n.	赛马的骑师；操作者	U2R2

K

kick up dust		扬起灰尘	U4R1

L

label	v.	标注	U1R2
launching pad		发射台；出发点	U2R2
lava	n.	火山岩浆；火山所喷出的熔岩	U2R1
layer	n.	层；层次	
	v.	把……分层堆放	U2R1
leave sb. alone		不打扰；不惊动	U1R1
leopard	n.	美洲豹	U4R1
liftoff	n.	发射	U1R2
likewise	ad.	同样	U5R1
line… with…		用……铺满……	U2R1
lingo	n.	行话，术语	U6R1
lottery	n.	彩票	U1R2
loyal	a.	忠诚的	U3R1

GLOSSARY

M

maize	n.	玉米	U7R2
make a difference		有影响；有关系	U7R2
mission	n.	使命，任务	U4R1
modify	v.	修改；修饰	U7R2
multiple	n.	倍数	U1R2
mystical	a.	神秘的	U1R2
mythology	n.	神话	U1R2

N

nutritional	a.	营养的，滋养的	U7R2

O

omen	n.	预兆，征兆	U1R2
opportunity	n.	机会	U4R2
oven	n.	炉，灶	U2R1
overall	a.	全部的	U3R2

P

passion	n.	热情	U4R1
passionate	a.	热情的	U4R1
paste	v.	张贴；裱糊；用浆糊粘	U2R1
personality	n.	个性；品格	U1R1
pest	n.	害虫；有害之物	U7R2
pesticide	n.	杀虫剂	U7R2
pile up		积累；堆放起来	U2R1
platter	n.	大浅盘	U2R1
plural	a.	复数的	U6R2
pop up		突然出现	U6R2
prominent	a.	显著的	U3R1
protest	v.	抗议；断言	U7R1
psychologist	n.	心理学家	U1R1
purity	n.	纯度；纯洁；纯净；纯粹	U1R1

R

range from... to...		在……和……之间变动；从……延伸到……	U3R2
raw	a.	生的；未加工的	U5R1
react to		对……做出反应	U3R1
regarding	prep.	关于；至于	U1R2
registration	n.	登记；注册	U2R2
restful	a.	宁静的；安静的	U1R1
restless	a.	焦躁不安的	U3R1
reveal	v.	揭露	U3R1
rhino	n.	犀牛	U4R1
roar	v.	咆哮	U4R1

S

savor	v.	尽情享受	U5R2
seasoning	n.	调料	U5R1
secrecy	n.	保密	U6R1
set a record		创造记录	U2R2
set out on a journey		启程	U1R2
share with		和……分享	U4R2
shorthand	n.	速写	U6R1
shovel	v.	铲	U2R1
show up		显露	U6R1
shrewd	a.	精明的；精于盘算的	U8R2
so long		好久	U1R2
soybean	n.	大豆；黄豆	U7R2
species	n.	物种；种类	U7R1
spectacular	a.	壮观的；惊人的	U2R2
spectator	n.	观众；旁观者	U2R2
spray... with...		用……喷在……上	U6R1
starch	n.	淀粉	U7R2
stern	a.	严厉的	U3R1
stimulate	v.	鼓舞，激励	U1R1
substantial	a.	大量的	U5R2
symbolically	ad.	象征性地	U1R1

GLOSSARY

T

therapy	n.	治疗	U3R2
throw out		逐出	U1R2
trait	n.	品质	U3R1
transmit	v.	传送	U6R1
tread	v.	行走	U8R1
tribe	n.	部落	U4R2
turtle	n.	龟	U3R2

U

undergrowth	n.	下层灌木丛	U8R1
unity	n.	团结；一致	U1R2
universally	ad.	普遍地	U1R2
unpredictable	a.	不可预知的	U2R2

V

vendor	n.	小贩	U5R2

W

wear	n.	磨损；耗损	U8R1
wicked	a.	邪恶的	U8R2
work out		锻炼	U2R2

Z

zigzag	v.	使成之字形；使曲折行进	U2R2